SCRIPTURE
AND TRADITION

A Survey of the Controversy

GABRIEL MORAN, F.S.C.

HERDER AND HERDER

1963
HERDER AND HERDER   NEW YORK
232 Madison Avenue, New York 16, N.Y.

Nihil obstat:
> Frederick J. Crowley
> Censor librorum

Imprimatur:
> † Robert F. Joyce
> Bishop of Burlington
> May 24, 1963

62535

CONTENTS

CONTENT

Foreword

THIS work which I am happy to preface belongs in the best tradition of what deserves to be called mediating theology. While some theologians feel the urge to strike out toward advanced positions, knowing that these may well become the conservative positions of tomorrow, others are concerned with preserving in the present the safe positions of the past, knowing also that by so doing they may incur the reproach of being outmoded. Between these two viewpoints—and I willingly admit that I belong to the first—a third type has recognized its vocation in the sympathetic investigation of both wings and in the effort to induce them to meet in a center.

The present book on tradition is a significant contribution to this mediation between two differing views in the current controversy among Catholic theologians on the relative importance of holy Scripture and holy tradition. The risk taken by the author is obviously that he may invite answers or even attacks from both sides. Mediators are always exposed to blows. In this case, however, I believe that exponents of both positions will find his mediation extremely well-informed, amiable, and fair to all, even if they feel, as I do, that some of the urbane criticism made by Brother Gabriel Moran is aimed at themselves.

Yet it may be possible to ask a preliminary question: is conciliation possible in this case? Precisions and distinctions of the meanings of terms may indeed bring the two understandings of Scripture and tradition nearer to each other; clarity of expres-

7

sion and factual accuracy will always help a discussion avoid the quicksands of mutual misinterpretation. Yet theological disagreements may have deeper roots than diverse semantic and historical emphases.

I suspect that behind the recent exchanges of views on tradition and Scripture there lie two very different concepts of the work and method of theology, each of which, possibly, has its own validity. If such is the case, conciliation is ultimately not feasible. There is room, in the large house of Catholicity, for several theologies. And, at this time at least, authoritative pronouncements to solve the problem of tradition would prematurely end one of the most fruitful processes that has taken place in theology: the confrontation of theological methods until one, or perchance both, die of exhaustion.

This raises a further question: what are the limits of conciliation in theology? Brother Gabriel has understood his task as consisting, first, in the objective presentation of the evidence as it is explained in a number of works of varying length, depth, and scope, and second, in an estimate of how near the positions really are to each other. The first task is fulfilled with such care that readers may hesitate to decide which side the author favors, or even if he favors either of them. The second task naturally calls for critical judgment by the author of both positions, at least in their sharpest formulations. Conciliation as an attempt to find a basic equivalence for diverging formulas is a necessary task. But full conciliation requires an evaluation of the different positions, not only in their formulations and conscious purposes but also in their more remote implications. I myself think that the implications of the notion that Scripture and tradition are two partial sources of faith are ultimately destructive of both

Scripture and tradition as the sacramental channels of the word of God. If this is correct, the limits of possible mediation and conciliation will soon be reached. And the fact that such a theology still dominates popular accounts of the matter does not protect it from the doctrinal deviations that may threaten it.

The attempt at conciliation has therefore certain inherent limits. Yet it is worth making, if only to test the theologies involved. If, as I have suggested, the main interpretations at stake manifest two types of theological method, mediating theology represents a third methodological type. I am very grateful to Brother Gabriel Moran for a fascinating demonstration of how this type works. His contribution to the current debate is that of a peacemaker, and it will help soften the sharp angles of controversy. It will also acquaint the cultured public with an important theological discussion. At a time when both Catholic and Protestant thoughts converge on the meaning of tradition for the Church, it will become a valuable addition to the library of ecumenism.

GEORGE H. TAVARD
Mount Mercy College
Pittsburgh, Pennsylvania

SCRIPTURE AND TRADITION

Introduction

DIVINE revelation is contained in holy Scripture and in sacred tradition. This statement has been made innumerable times in classes of theology, and it can be found in any standard theological manual. That it should be is not surprising because the statement represents a defined truth of the Catholic faith. In connection with this simple truth, however, a profound theological problem has long persisted, namely, the relationship of Scripture and tradition. If there are two sources of revelation, the question immediately arises of whether the contents of these two are exclusive of one another, partially overlap, or are identical. This question has been widely discussed and debated among contemporary theologians.[1]

The problem of the relationship between Scripture and tradition is, of course, not a new one; it is one of those fundamental questions that has its roots deep in the history of Christianity. In the last few years, however, it has become the center of new and intensive study. Many works on the concept of tradition originated in the nineteenth century and the early twentieth, but as the second half of this century opened, there began to appear a widening stream of material on tradition and tradition's relation to Scripture. Under the influence of several different factors, this stream of material has continued to broaden during the past ten years.

The present work is an attempt to bring together the main issues which have developed in the last few years. The present time would seem to be opportune for undertaking such a study. I have said that the amount of writing on this question has greatly increased in the last few years; for that reason, it might seem that more time is needed before an appraisal can be made. However, a survey of the most recent studies on this topic indicates that the lines of the argument have become fairly well determined. Many scholarly works are in the process of composition and many more will be needed—and probably a declaration of the Church's magisterium—before a full and clear answer can be given to this question; but at least an agreement now seems to have emerged on where the disagreement lies.

Most of the writing which has recently been done on this subject has been confined to theological journals.[2] Despite the excellence of many of these articles, it usually happens that only a part of the question is treated; in the course of a short essay, an author usually defends one of the answers without bringing together all that is involved in the question. My purpose in this work is to let each side speak for itself, and then, after the evidence has been set forth on both sides of the question, I will attempt to draw some conclusions on the points of agreement or disagreement and to suggest the direction in which the solution seems to lie.

Since the problem we are to deal with is so fundamental to Catholic theology, it is necessarily extensive and complex. And although the relationship of Scripture and tradition is the only matter under consideration here, such a fundamental question inevitably touches upon numerous other theological problems. I will make no attempt here to answer these other questions; but some indication will be given of how the central problem of this book is related to some of these other theological issues, such as, for example, the development of dogma. It is only by setting the question in its proper context that the problem can be fully grasped and the differing answers and opinions understood.

My intention is to show what ideas have emerged in recent years which may clarify the notion of tradition. A detailed historical study is beyond the scope of this work, although I recognize that such historical research is necessary for a full solution. Historical considerations will play a major role in the presentation of the problem, but my direct concern will be with the conclusions and interpretations of the best recent historical studies.[3]

I have also chosen to limit this study to the writings of the past ten years; my choice of this decade is not purely arbitrary since approximately the year 1951 marks a definite milestone in the development of the question. With the definition of the Assumption of the Blessed Virgin, new light was shed on the notion of tradition and the relation of tradition to Scripture. The period following upon *Munificentissimus Deus,* therefore, constitutes a logical starting point for this inquiry.

Chapter 1

Is There a Constitutive Tradition?

"The Council is aware that this truth and teaching are contained in written books and in the unwritten traditions that the Apostles received from Christ himself or that were handed on as it were from hand to hand, from the Apostles under the inspiration of the Holy Spirit, and so have come down to us."[4]

Any discussion of the notion of tradition and the sources of revelation must take careful account of the authoritative declaration of the Fourth Session of the Council of Trent since this is the clearest statement of the Church's magisterium on the meaning of tradition within the Catholic faith. The definition just quoted is in one sense a conclusion to the whole question; on the other hand, it is also a starting point for the understanding of the theologian. Not only is it permissible to speculate on the meaning of such a definition—it is an urgent necessity to determine exactly what Trent has defined on this matter. The definition of Trent has been brought under closest scrutiny within the ten-year period to be studied here, and the question has been raised of whether post-Tridentine theology has completely understood the decree of Trent on the meaning of tradition. Many scholars have suggested that the notion of tradition is more complex than a number of standard treatments would indicate.

Most Catholics would probably view tradition as a rather simple and uncomplicated idea. They may have had it defined for them as "the collection of revealed truths which the Church has received through the Apostles in addition to inspired Scripture and which it preserves by uninterrupted continuity of the apostolic teaching office."[5] In the thinking of many theologians, especially since the nineteenth century, this definition is not a happy one, and certainly it is not a complete one.

The author of the above quotation proceeds to embody his definition in the following proposition:

> Tradition is a source of revelation distinct from Scripture and goes beyond the data of Scripture. This is a *dogma of faith* from the Council of Trent as quoted above and the Vatican Council. The first part of the proposition states the existence of tradition in general and consequently includes inherent tradition; the second part refers specifically to constitutive tradition.[6]

The author expresses no doubt that the existence of constitutive tradition is a defined truth of the Catholic faith, and yet precisely this point—the existence of constitutive tradition—has been the center of the debate in recent years. Obviously, Catholic theologians who deny the existence of such tradition have no intention of denying a dogma of faith; what they do deny is that the existence of constitutive tradition has been defined as an article of faith by the Council of Trent.

This is the question I shall examine: is there a constitutive tradition? From all appearances it is a simple question to which there would seem to be only two possible answers—yes or no. Before going any further with the question, however, the first task is to define in precise terms what is meant by *tradition* and more specifically what is meant by the phrase *constitutive tradition*.

The word *tradition* in its etymological meaning signifies a handing over. In Catholic theology, the word refers in its most general sense to the transmission of institutions, beliefs, and practices in the Church through the course of the centuries. With this broad meaning as a base, the word is used in several different ways.

We must first distinguish between active or subjective tradition and passive or objective tradition. In speaking of the transmission of a body of material, one can refer to the material itself or to the act of transmission. The body of material, the set of beliefs and practices, the content of tradition we speak of as *objective* or *passive tradition*. On the other hand, when we wish to refer to the act of handing over or to the organ of transmission, we use the expression *subjective* or *active tradition*. All theologians agree that in some sense active tradition must be identified with the Church itself. Since the middle of the nineteenth century the word *tradition* has been used more and more in this sense, and great stress has been laid upon the magisterium and its close connection with tradition.[7] It would be a mistake, however, not to keep a clear distinction between passive tradition on the one hand and the magisterium and active tradition on the other.

Looking next at the content of tradition, one can further distinguish several kinds of (objective) tradition. According to the origin of the tradition, it may be called divine-apostolic, human-apostolic, or ecclesiastical. By divine-apostolic tradition we mean the truths which were revealed by God to the Apostles through the person of Christ or by the direct working of the Holy Spirit. The origin of this tradition is the Apostles, precisely insofar as they were Apostles, the transmitters of the revealed word, the source and font of all revelation. A human-apostolic tradition, in contrast, is one which originated with the Apostles but is not part of revelation. The Apostles were not only the source of revelation; they were also the first pastors of the Church. In erecting the Church in its fully human structure, they necessarily set down many things which did not have their origin in a divine revelation. It is then possible to speak of apostolic traditions without referring to revelation, and this is what would be meant by a human-apostolic tradition. Finally, if we wish to speak of traditions that have originated in the Church in postapostolic times, we generally refer to ecclesiastical tradition. Since revelation closed with the apostolic age, it is clear that ecclesiastical tradition in this sense never refers to a revealed truth.[8]

A different and simpler way of distinguishing the content matter of tradition is to designate a tradition as either dogmatic or disciplinary. When we use the term *dogmatic tradition,* we refer to revealed doctrines, the religious truths made known by God before the death of the last Apostle. The term *disciplinary tradition* could be used of any practice which has long existed in the Church; this would include, for example, liturgical rites and ceremonies. Disciplinary tradition could be either apostolic or postapostolic, but in either case it would not be part of divine revelation.[9]

Last of all, we may speak of the different ways in which (dogmatic) tradition is contained in revelation. If we ask where and how a dogmatic tradition is found, we necessarily bring up the question of tradition's relationship to holy Scripture. There are three possible ways that a truth in tradition could be related to the Scriptures. First, traditions which are explicit in Holy Scripture may be described as *inherent tradition*. Second, if a tradition is implicitly contained in the Scriptures, it is called *declarative tradition*. Third, a *constitutive tradition* would be one which exists separate from holy Scripture; it would be a revealed truth which is not contained even implicitly in Scripture.[10] Therefore, inquiries into constitutive tradition refer to objective, divine-apostolic, dogmatic, extrascriptural, revealed truth. It is the notion of constitutive tradition with this precisely defined meaning that is at the center of present discussions on the meaning of tradition.[11]

To ask whether there is a constitutive tradition, therefore, is to ask whether or not Scripture "contains" all revealed truth either explicitly or implicitly.[12] Those who deny that there is a constitutive tradition are denying that there is an independent body of revealed truths existing apart from the Scriptures; they are asserting that all dogmatic tradition is declarative or inherent in Scripture. It should be carefully noted that this is not a denial of tradition but a denial of one form of tradition. No one denies that the existence of objective, divine-apostolic, dogmatic tradition is an article of faith. The sole question at issue is whether this objective tradition contains truths which are extrascriptural, that is, truths which are not contained at all in holy Scripture.[13]

To many Catholics the very raising of this question would be incomprehensible; to them it could hardly be more obvious that there are dogmatic truths which are not contained in Scripture. Our first consideration, then, must concern the validity of the question itself. Obviously, to understand properly why many theologians deny the existence of constitutive tradition requires some attention to the reasons which have led to this denial; whatever opinion one may have about the answer to this question, one should first seek to understand what these theologians are saying and why they are saying it.

Up until 1950 some Catholic theologians denied that the Assumption of the Blessed Virgin could be defined as an article of faith because it was impossible to trace the doctrine to the apostolic age.[14] Yet on November 1 of that year Pope Pius XII solemnly proclaimed the Assumption as a dogma of faith.[15] The Pope, it would seem, did not proceed from the historical evidence of the first Christian centuries but worked according to a regressive method from the consensus of belief of the Church to the necessity of the doctrine in revelation. The definition of the dogma was the occasion for many Catholic theologians to examine more carefully the question of doctrinal development. This was no new problem, of course; much had been written concerning the development of dogma during the preceding century. But although the problem did not suddenly emerge in the year 1950, the bull on the Assumption did provide a striking example of the problem of development and the need for serious consideration of all that is involved in that problem. The continued examination of the whole subject of dogmatic development has led some to conclude that if extrascriptural tradition is not sufficient to explain the development, if indeed its supposition does not even make the problem easier to solve, then it is superfluous to suppose its existence at all.[16] It is thought by these theologians that what is needed is a good theory of doctrinal development and that such a theory would dispense us from having recourse to the supposition of an extrascriptural tradition.[17]

Modern biblical studies have in their turn indicated the close relationship between Scripture and tradition. A point which has been strongly emphasized in recent years is that the New Testament is the written crystallization or precipitate of the apostolic *paradosis*. The clearer perception of this fact has had a profound effect among both Catholic and Protestant theologians on the concept of the relationship of Scripture and tradition.[18] With emphasis placed upon Scripture as the apostolic witness to revelation, the Bible, which was at times looked upon in some Catholic circles—at least by implication—as an accidental collection of parts of revelation, has been given a more exalted position. As a result, many would maintain that Scripture is not a mere part of revelation but that it contains at least in general fashion the whole of revelation.[19] Far from being a haphazard collection, the Scriptures should be looked upon as "the adequate objectivity of the primal consciousness of the Church."[20] In this view the contents of Scripture and tradition are identical, Scripture being the written form of early tradition. The present-day conception of Scripture, therefore, easily lends itself to the affirmation that the whole of revelation is implicit in Scripture and that there is no need for the existence of a constitutive tradition.

While additional studies of Scripture and tradition were being made, the Council of Trent was also the object of renewed and intensive study. Great impetus was given to the debate on constitutive tradition by the publication of the work of Geiselmann in 1956.[21] As I have pointed out, any opinion on the nature of tradition must be reconcilable with the Tridentine decree. That decree, in fact, has become the focal point of the whole debate, and I shall later investigate in some detail the differing interpretations of it. What I would like to stress here is that the very possibility of raising the question is dependent upon an interpretation

23

of Trent which differs from that most often made in the six-teenth, seventeenth, and eighteenth centuries.

Before examining both sides of this question and the evidence which is offered in support of each answer, it would be best to clarify a few expressions which sometimes hinder a clear under-standing of the problem. It is necessary to have clearly in mind the signification which these expressions have in Catholic the-ology; otherwise the main point can be lost in semantic con-fusion. One of the difficulties arising out of the question of the Scripture-tradition relationship is that stress can be laid on one or the other of the two poles so that a passage taken out of con-text may sound as if the opposite pole is being minimized or denied altogether. Compare, for example, these two statements:

Revelation is handed down to us with the direct authority of God only in the canonical books. . . . The Church in her magisterium is the first to recognize that she is subject to the word of God as contained in the Bible.[22]

The most superior source of Christianity is not the word of the Bible but the living word of the Church's proclamation of the faith. . . . The Bible is and always will be a valuable source of material, but not the primary source of Christian faith.[23]

The clash in formulas of these two statements is certainly strik-ing, but the actual opinions of the two writers are not so far apart as it would at first appear. It is not irrelevant that the first state-ment is made in connection with the positive principles that can be attributed to the reformers; the second statement is taken from a treatment of the limits of biblical criticism. In understanding the following expressions one cannot therefore rely solely on verbal analysis but must derive the meaning of the expressions from the contexts in which they appear.

Some Catholic writers today maintain that the expression, "the sufficiency of Scripture" (*scriptura sola*) was not a discovery of the reformers but that the formula is a genuinely Catholic principle.[24] To other Catholic theologians, the phrase *scriptura sola* carries dangerous connotations and ought not to be used. But whether or not it is prudent—and, more basically, correct— to use the expression, it simply does not mean the same thing in Catholic writing as it does in Protestant. No Catholic theologian advocates a *scriptura sola* position in the sense in which the reformers used the expression.[25] It is not merely that the Catholic needs the infallible magisterium to settle the more difficult problems of exegesis and to elicit the hidden truths of Scripture, but rather that for the Catholic *all* revealed truth comes to him through the teaching of the Church. This remains true whether Scripture contains all of revelation or only a part of it.[26] If then a Catholic writer speaks of the "sufficiency of Scripture," he clearly does not mean that Scripture is sufficient for the Catholic religion; what he does mean is that Scripture is materially complete or sufficient, that Scripture contains all of the revelation the Church teaches. He is denying the existence of a constitutive tradition but he is not denying tradition. He is asserting that the contents of Scripture and tradition are identical.

Another idea which has caused confusion in Catholic circles is that holy Scripture is the authoritative norm for the Church's teaching.[27] Concerning this expression, one theologian asks, "When it is said that all Catholic dogmatic teaching has Scripture as its norm, are we not suggesting that we have given up

Tradition and have accepted the position of the Reformers?"[28] It would seem, however, that the word *norm,* like the word *tradition,* can have several different meanings. When a Protestant writer insists that Scripture must be the authoritative norm for the Church's teaching, and when one Catholic writer agrees that Scripture is a binding and authoritative norm while yet another Catholic writer says that the norm for Catholic belief is the teaching of the magisterium, it is obvious that the word *norm* can embrace a number of meanings.[29]

In order to clarify the terminology, it is important to keep in mind the distinction made above between active and passive tradition. Objective tradition, the content of faith, is found in the apostolic tradition; since apostolic tradition contains all the revealed truths of the Catholic faith, it is, as such, the norm of faith with respect to content. This is true regardless of whether that apostolic tradition is contained partly or totally in Scripture. While Pope Pius XII spoke of the Church's magisterium as the "proximate and universal norm for every theologian," he also made clear that the role of the magisterium is as guardian and interpreter of revealed truth (as found in the apostolic tradition) but not as a separate source of truth.[30] Therefore, both apostolic tradition and the magisterium can each be called the norm of faith. To speak of the magisterium as a norm is to refer to its directive role as interpreter of the deposit of revelation; to use the word *norm* with reference to apostolic tradition is to speak of the objective, material-content norm of faith.[31] With this distinction in mind, it is not difficult to grasp what a Catholic theologian means when he says that Scripture is the sufficient, authoritative, and binding norm of the Church's teaching. This is but another way of asserting that the whole of divine revelation given to the

Apostles—which everyone must admit is the norm of faith in the sense we have just defined—is contained in holy Scripture.

Finally, there is another ambiguous expression closely allied to the previous one which can create difficulties in the discussion of this question. Some theologians refer to the Church as subordinate to Scripture or as a true servant to the word of Scripture.[32] Although it may be possible to "agree with the Protestants that the magisterium exercises only a subordinate role to Scripture,"[33] it is also necessary to specify exactly in what sense the words *superior* and *subordinate* are being used. The distinction invoked in the previous section is applicable here also. As far as the content of revelation is concerned, the magisterium is subordinate to apostolic tradition; it is from the apostolic period that the Church draws all of the faith she lives by. Thus Daniélou could agree with Cullmann that the apostolic period is unique, and that the Apostles can have no successors as Apostles, that is, insofar as they were the source of revelation. On the other hand, insofar as the Apostles were the first pastors of the Church with authority to safeguard and interpret revelation, then apostolic successors are both possible and necessary.[34] Therefore, since the apostolic period is the unique source of faith, the Scriptures can in one sense—with respect to content—be called superior to the Church, and in this sense we may speak of the Church as subordinating herself to the Scriptures. On the other hand, since the Church continues to present and interpret revelation through every period of history with an authority derived from Christ, the Church can be called superior to the written word—with respect to clarity of presentation. Of both Scripture and the Church we can say that it is a supreme and infallible authority.

There is a delicate balance to be maintained in this regard, and it is somewhat dangerous to speak of *either* Church *or* Scripture as superior to the other. Once the proper balance is lost, once the reciprocal relationship of Church and Scripture is overlooked and the two infallible authorities go their separate ways, the problem of which is the higher authority must eventually arise. All Catholic theologians today are interested in maintaining a real organic unity of Scripture, Church, and tradition. It is for the sake of better establishing that unity—according to their reasoning—that many theologians deny the existence of constitutive tradition. We must now consider the evidence in support of that position.

Chapter 2

The Negative View

WE shall examine in this chapter the evidence offered by those who deny the existence of a constitutive tradition. The burden of proof in this debate seems to rest on them because—whether it is justified or not—the existence of a tradition containing extra-scriptural truths is the popular conception which has been dominant in the Church of both the recent past and the present. Most of the theologians to be cited here view the present movement as a simple step forward in the clarification of dogma; one of them goes so far as to call the theory of two partial sources of faith a "now antiquated legend" and "a mistake which scholars have exposed time and again."[35] Nevertheless, the "legend" does live on and it is necessary for these theologians to support their contention with proof.

One of the main objections which would arise in the minds of many Catholics to the denial of extrascriptural tradition would be that it is a dangerous innovation and an imprudent step toward reconciliation with Protestantism. Not only would that charge be unjustified, say these theologians, but it would be a complete misconception of what history reveals: "This modification of current theological teaching is not indeed an innovation so much as a return to pre-Tridentine tradition in classical theology, which is more in accord with Patristic thought and of which St. Thomas is the chief representative."[36] What is called traditional and what is called new depend on one's point of departure. It is true that constitutive tradition has had its place in Catholic theology for several centuries, but this does not necessarily make it the traditional view or the Catholic view. In defending itself against the reformers, post-Tridentine theology was led into an error similar to that of Protestantism—the equating of revelation with the canonical text. But whereas the Protestants accepted only Scripture, Catholic theologians supposed Scripture incomplete and brought in tradition to supplement it.[37] To determine what the proper role of tradition has been and ought to be in the life of the Church, it is necessary to study the notion of tradition as it has existed and as it has developed throughout the centuries.

The New Testament is the written form of the apostolic *paradosis,* the distilled essence of apostolic teaching. Revelation first existed in an oral form, but as time went on the Church put this testimony into writing, and gradually the Scriptures grew out of the life of the Church.[38] Therefore, in the first ages of the Church, "apostolic tradition" could only mean the Church's understanding of the mystery of Christ; and the Scriptures were the written witness of that understanding. A rigid distinction between Scripture on the one hand and tradition on the other would have been quite unthinkable, the former being the precipitate of the latter. When she fixed the canon of Scripture, the Church was in effect separating spurious tradition from genuine. Her decision on which were the inspired books seems to have been largely determined by measuring their doctrine against her actual teaching. The Scriptures and the Church existed at that time and continued to exist in a reciprocal relationship.[39]

The modern idea of a constitutive tradition would seem to imply that there were traditions secretly handed down over long periods of time before emerging into history. But "besides the fact that the testimony of the Fathers expressly contradicts the idea of an esoteric tradition, the supposition would be completely lacking in historical plausibility."[40] It was precisely this hidden tradition which the Church was fighting in Gnosticism.[41] Where the Fathers do refer to traditions outside of Scripture, it is in speaking of liturgical and disciplinary practices, not of a stream of revealed truth flowing parallel to Scripture. This seems to be the case even with St. Basil, who often refers to extrascriptural traditions.[42]

Two writers of the patristic period are most often cited as witnesses to the unity of Scripture and tradition in the early Church, Irenaeus and Vincent of Lérins.

With Irenaeus, we have one of the earliest and clearest testimonies of the proper relationship of Scripture and tradition. Studies of this saint in modern times indicate that for him there is "one tradition, apostolic in source and ecclesiastical in transmission," which is the faithful interpretation of the Scriptures. For Irenaeus the division of revelation into two partial sources would have been quite unthinkable.[43]

Vincent of Lérins was a witness in particular to the completeness of holy Scripture; he maintained that all the truths of the Catholic faith are to be found in the Scriptures. At the same time, however, he was also insistent that because of the many possible interpretations of Scripture, an authoritative interpretation by the

31

Church was necessary. This is what Vincent meant by tradition: the Church's understanding by which Scripture is clarified and explained. Revelation, according to Vincent, is not divided between two sources; it is contained totally in the written words of Scripture and totally in the oral form of the Church's teaching.[44]

Although other early writers of the Church are not so explicit as Irenaeus and Vincent of Lérins in their exposition of the Scripture-tradition relationship, the same general outlook and tendency are discernible. God's saving word was to be found in Scripture, but Scripture was to be read and interpreted only in the light of the Church's traditional teaching.[45] Gradually, over the course of the centuries, a whole set of commentaries grew up about the sacred books. It should be noted that the exegesis which was used in these commentaries and meditations was not restricted to the purely logical and philosophical. As late as the thirteenth century the study of theology was called *sacra scriptura* or *sacra pagina*. These terms did not signify a merely scientific analysis of the sacred text; there was always included with the biblical texts the earlier writings on the Scriptures.[46]

A problem began to arise in the Middle Ages when words like *inspirare* and *revelare* were not restricted to the canonical books. This ambiguous situation was realized by St. Thomas, who generally used these and similar words only when referring to biblical texts. To the Fathers and Doctors, he gave the status of commentators and guardians of the true sense of Scripture. At the beginning of the *Summa Theologiae* (I, q. 1, art. 8, ad. 2), St. Thomas distinguishes three levels of authority in theology. The first level is the extrinsic authority of philosophy; the second is the proper but probable authority of the early Fathers; the third, holy Scripture, is the one which possesses "proper and necessary authority." The only conclusive argument is one drawn from holy Scripture; there is no alternative source from which to draw arguments that have "necessary authority."[47]

For all the Scholastic theologians, then, down through the fourteenth century the basic charter was Scripture; the texts of the early Fathers and commentators had their place as part of the living interpretative organ. "Tradition, considered as an original and independent source of Christian doctrine, was unknown to the theology of that era."[48] Yet all was not so simple and clear as these last words might indicate. Although there was no talk of a separate source of faith, and although it was still affirmed that Scripture was the basis for all doctrine, yet the fourteenth and fifteenth centuries were slowly drawing away from Scripture itself. As speculation and piety tended to separate from Scripture, the idea of the Church became blurred. The patristic idea of the Church as a mighty mystery and an organic whole gradually changed into the Nominalist conception of a mere *collectio fidelium*. Whereas the Church and the Scriptures had been looked upon as inseparable notions, there now arose considerations— purely speculative at first—of what would happen if Scripture and Church contradicted each other on some point of doctrine. With William of Ockham the radical separation of the two was effected, and the problem had to arise eventually as to which was the superior authority, holy Writ or holy Church.[49]

Luther, who had been trained in the theology of Ockham and Biel, was faced with this false option of the primacy of Scripture or the primacy of Church. When he made his choice he reverted to Scholastic terminology in proclaiming the supremacy of Scripture, but at the same time he accepted the recent identification of revelation with the words of the canonical books. As we have already indicated, the saying "Scripture alone" was not new with Luther; what was new was the idea that Scripture was the mere text, which could be understood apart from the authoritative interpretation of the Church.[50] In the face of this Protestant attack, the Council of Trent met, and the stage was set for the defense of the revelation which is contained in "written books and unwritten traditions."

Of the decree of Trent on Scripture and tradition, a Protestant writer states, "Against Scripture alone, Trent pitted Scripture and tradition . . . but forsook tradition in the act of defining it, for tradition was on the side of biblical authority."[51] It may be questioned, however, whether this is what Trent actually did, and whether a division of revelation into Scripture and tradition was what Trent intended to define. Some insist today that the story is not so simple as post-Tridentine theologians often took it to be. An understanding of the decree must be sought in a study of the Acts of the Council and of its sixteenth-century background.[52]

In approaching the Council of Trent's discussions on this matter, one is faced immediately with the problem that the word *tradition* is not carefully defined from the beginning. To read twentieth-century definitions of tradition into the sixteenth century would therefore distort the historical picture. In the first reports on tradition at the Council, the phrases "traditions of the Apostles" and "traditions of the Church" were used, but without any precise definitions. The Jesuit Claude Lejay clarified the discussion by distinguishing between traditions *quae ad fidem pertinent* and all other traditions, but even after this, disciplinary and liturgical traditions continued to be mixed into the discussions on dogmatic traditions.[53]

By the end of the first general congregations in February, 1542, an agreement had been reached on three points: there are apostolic traditions which are truly doctrinal; tradition refers to the oral transmission of the teaching of Christ; and the Council would not enumerate such traditions.[54] The drafting of the decree was then begun, and it was completed by March 22. The decree stated that the glad tidings of Jesus Christ "are contained partly in the written books, and partly in unwritten traditions which the Apostles received from Christ's own lips or which, under the inspiration of the Holy Spirit were by them, as it were, passed down to us from hand to hand." The decree goes on to add that the unwritten traditions, preserved by the continuity of the Church, are to be received *pari pietatis affectu,* that is, with the same reverence as one has for Scripture.

It is on the words *partly-partly* in the decree that Geiselmann has concentrated his attention in his study of Trent. The expression is evidently the one Cardinal del Monte used in the first congregation of February 12, when he said, "The truth of God is contained partly in written books and partly in unwritten traditions." Geiselmann has tried to discover the origin of the expression *partly-partly,* and concludes that it is a recent pre-Tridentine expression first used in A. Traversari's translation of Pseudo-Dionysius's *De Hierarchica Ecclesiastica.*[55] Other pre-Tridentine writers, among them Fisher and Eck, picked up the expression, and it quickly became an autonomous formula; it seemed to be the most appropriate and effective refutation of the reformers' "Scripture alone" theory. Revelation, said these Catholic theologians, is divided between two sources; part of revelation is found in Scripture, but the rest is contained only in oral tradition, that is, in truths handed down from apostolic times in addition to the Scripture. The Bible itself, it was said, testifies to this fact: "There are many other things which Jesus did that are not written down in this book . . ." (John 20:30).[56]

There would seem to have been a difference of opinion on this matter in the period before Trent, but how great that difference was in the era preceding the Council and the Council itself is not at all easy to determine. Geiselmann has tried to show that there was a double current of thought in that period, and that the second channel of thought showed up in the Council to produce a minority reaction to the partly-partly formula.[57]

At any rate, there were at least two dissentng voices in the Council which opposed the suggested formula. In the congregation of February 26, G. Nacchianti, bishop of Chioggia, protested that all truths necessary to salvation are found in Scripture. His opinion, however, was rejected by the other Fathers of the Council.[58] After the first draft of the decree had been formulated, a similar objection was made by Bonucci, the general of the Servites. He objected to the partly-partly formula because, said he, "It is my judgment that all evangelical truth is written, hence not part of it." One might have expected violent accusations of Protestantism by the other Fathers, but nothing of the kind happened; "Neither the Acts of the Council nor the diaries breathe a word of such an accusation."[59] To all appearances, however, Bonucci's plea was unsuccessful; there was no reaction at all recorded among the Fathers of the Council.

Six days later the final draft of the decree appeared, and along with other modifications the words *partly-partly* (*partim-partim*) had been replaced by the word *and* (*et*). The decree thus read: revelation is contained in written books and unwritten traditions. The single word *et* has become the center of controversy in recent times. Up to this point in the Acts of the Council, the facts seem generally clear. With the redaction of the April 8 decree, however, not one word is recorded explaining why the change was made or how it is to be interpreted.

This issue may seem small,[60] but it has taken on great importance in discussions today and has been the subject of much speculation. After describing the debate on the formula *pari pietatis affectu,* Jedin concludes that "at the very latest moment, *partim-partim* was replaced by *et;* thus the wishes of the minority were after all met in a decisive passage of the decree."[61] This is the interpretation favored by many contemporary theologians. The Council was faced with a double current of thought on this question, one insisting that revelation is divided between Scripture and tradition, the other maintaining that revelation is entirely in Scripture as interpreted by tradition. As in many other such controversies, the Council did not wish to choose for one school or the other. Therefore, to the second question which we may ask —what the *et* signifies—Geiselmann gives the answer, "Nothing, nothing at all. With the word *et,* the Council avoided a decision because the question was not yet ready for a final solution."[62]

The Council thus attended to its most immediate concern, the existence of oral tradition in opposition to the doctrine of the reformers. As for the further question of the relationship of the contents of unwritten traditions and written books, the Council left this question open to further discussion. The answer could not be given then because the question was not sufficiently well formulated.[63] Many present-day theologians would therefore summarize their interpretation of Trent in the following points.

The Council of Trent's primary concern was to oppose the *scriptura sola* doctrine of Protestantism. The Council had no intention of giving an exposition of the whole doctrine of tradition.[64] There is a great difficulty in defining the expression *apostolic tradition;* both dogmatic and disciplinary traditions are often mixed in the same discussion.[65] The Council declared that the Gospel is transmitted to us by a double means: written books, that is, the canonical books of Scripture, and unwritten traditions, that is, orally.[66] The initial wording of the decree seemed to indicate that the Gospel is divided between two sources. The final text was altered so as to read "written books and unwritten traditions," thereby avoiding the parallelism of the two-source theory.[67] Thus, the relationship of the contents of Scripture and tradition was not defined. There is a difference of opinion among these theologians on the exact intention of the Council, but in general they agree that at the very least the question is still open to discussion.[68]

Whatever Trent intended to define on the Scripture-tradition relationship, there is very little controversy about the interpretation of post-Tridentine theologians. Sixteenth-century theologians like Cano, Bellarmine, and Canisius, in stressing the equality of tradition and Scripture as opposed to the doctrine of the reformers, originated the modern two-source theory.[69] The classification of theological sources by Melchior Cano placed emphasis on tradition as an extrascriptural source of revelation and tended to put the Church, Scripture, and tradition into separate categories.[70] Thus, the theologians of the seventeenth and eighteenth centuries who thought they were agreeing with Trent were in reality assenting to the sixteenth-century misinterpretation of Trent. Theologians of the classical era sought proofs from tradition in the writings of the first three centuries, the "classic ideal of the church." Scripture, tradition, and Church were considered to be separate entities, each contributing its argument to the formulation of theological proofs.

The romantic era of the nineteenth century began to correct this notion of tradition, that is, tradition conceived of as a set of ideas contained in early patristic writing. In the nineteenth century, tradition was looked upon more as a living process which continues throughout the life of the Church. The theologians of Tübingen were most influential in this re-establishment of tradition in its proper role in the Church. Influenced by men like Lessing and Klüpfel, Johannes Möhler proposed that "the Gospel is totally in the living tradition." Nevertheless, despite both Franzelin's and Möhler's better understanding of tradition, the completely balanced outlook of Vincent of Lérins had not yet been attained. To Möhler it seemed sufficiently clear that Scripture was an incomplete account of revelation. Scripture appeared to him to be the written part of revelation which needs both interpretation and completion by the living tradition.[71]

The final step in restoring the balance was left to John Baptist Kuhn. He began his career as an exegete, and through his polemics against Strauss he came to see Scripture as the written crystallization of apostolic preaching. In his early work he followed Möhler's idea, that revelation is contained totally in tradition and partly in Scripture. By 1858, however, Kuhn had changed his position; he now held that revelation is contained totally in Scripture and totally in tradition. Scripture, he taught, is the distilled essence of the apostolic witness, and tradition is the Church's understanding of Scripture. Therefore, both Scripture and tradition mediate the whole Gospel, but each under a different form.[72]

While the Tübingen school was restoring the proper balance of Scripture and tradition on the Continent, a similar movement was under way in England. Cardinal Newman's ideas on the development of doctrine seem to have been influenced by the same line of thought. Newman took cognizance of the assertion of William Palmer, an Anglican, that Trent had avoided saying that revelation is contained partly in Scripture and partly in tradition.[73] In one famous passage, Newman wrote, "I am not aware that the later post-Tridentine writers deny that the whole Catholic faith may be proved from Scripture, though they would certainly maintain that it is not to be found on the surface of it, nor in such sense that it may be gained from Scripture without the aid of tradition."[74]

This broader view of tradition joined an increased awareness of magisterial teaching as the proximate norm of faith. The reunification of the theological sources which had been separated under the stress of the post-Reformation was now possible. Unfortunately, however, the work of these nineteenth-century theologians did not have an immediate or wide effect upon the early twentieth century. The popular conception was still that of proving doctrines from Scripture and from tradition; what could not be proved from Scripture could be proved by tracing the doctrine through the Fathers to apostolic times. As the twentieth century progressed, however, new consideration was given to the nature of tradition, the sources of revelation, and the development of dogma. And it is in the last ten years that the problem has emerged in clearest form.

This brief history of the question leads us to conclude that the early Church up until the Middle Ages did not separate Scripture and tradition as two sources of revelation. Scripture was the one book which contained God's word; the Scriptures were read, understood, and commented upon in the light of the Church's traditional teaching. On the other hand, in the late Middle Ages, a weakened concept of the Church tended to separate the Scriptures from tradition. Eventually a false opposition arose between the authority of the Church and the authority of sacred Scripture, with the Protestant reformers defending the supremacy of Scripture. Against the reformers, the Council of Trent defined that the written books are not the sole means of the transmission of God's revelation. The Council said that the revelation is also transmitted orally and that this oral tradition must be received as reverently as Scripture.

But the post-Tridentine era, not sufficiently removed from the late medieval dichotomy of Bible and Church, treated Scripture and tradition as two separate sources. It was thought that the Church preserved the Scriptures on the one hand and on the other the writings of the Fathers, wherein the oral traditions were to be found. However, in modern times, with the passing of the Protestant threat and an increased awareness of the notion of the Mystical Body, emphasis has been placed upon the Church's character as a living organism. In this viewpoint, Scripture and tradition are no longer seen as disjointed parts of a whole but rather as organically related to the living magisterium.

Thus, those who deny the existence of constitutive tradition and thereby maintain that revelation is contained wholly in Scripture as understood by the living tradition under the guidance of the magisterium assert that they are merely carrying the century-old movement to its logical conclusion. With the present realization of the nature of the Church, the existence of constitutive tradition has been rendered superfluous.

The last paragraph of the historical survey above leads us into a consideration of constitutive tradition from a doctrinal viewpoint. Those who deny constitutive tradition contend that theirs is not merely a negative position and that it affects more than one point of doctrine. The elimination of constitutive tradition, they believe, is a necessary step forward in the proper understanding of the doctrines of Scripture, tradition, and Church.

One of the common complaints of Protestant critics of Catholicism is that the Church does not give the Bible the central position it demands. They claim that instead of stressing that Scripture is the word of God, "It suits modern Roman apologetic, in its disparagement of Scripture in the interests of tradition, to magnify the incidental character of the Scripture into a positive defect and imperfection."[75] This attitude, the Protestants claim, is an insult to the Apostles and to the Bible. Some Catholic writers, it is true, have given the impression at times that they look on the Bible as an accidental collection of fragments;[76] while it is always granted that God's word is important, it is sometimes suggested that such a book is not really necessary for Catholicism since the Catholic Church could get along well enough without holy Scripture.

This view of the Scriptures, many today insist, was not that of the early Fathers nor that of the great medieval theologians, and it has never been the official attitude of the Church; she has always treated the Bible with the greatest reverence and solemnity. In her official teaching the Church always turns back to the Scriptures to reflect upon them, so that even in a doctrinal definition such as the Assumption Scripture is given as the "ultimate foundation."[77] Modern scriptural study, as I noted previously, has brought out the nature of Scripture as the written form, the crystallization, of the apostolic witness to God's full revelation in Christ. Holy Scripture is the memorial which the Apostles left to a future age. To think that it is not a perfect and sufficient memorial of the apostolic tradition would be doing an injustice to both the Apostles and the Scriptures.[78]

Whether there could have been a Catholic Church without a Bible is a question one might speculate upon. In actual fact, of course, Scripture has always played a central role in the Church's life since apostolic times. There is no problem of opposition between the two authorities once it is realized that they are reciprocally related. The Bible is a book which can be correctly read and understood only in the Church, and the Church, for her part, has the mission and the authority to preserve Scripture and pronounce on its meaning. The Bible is *the* book of the Church, the source of her doctrine; it cannot be separated from her being.[79]

There are some who fear that the denial of constitutive tradition is a movement to exalt Scripture at the expense of tradition. But the paradoxical conclusion is that the role of tradition is being given its truest and deepest meaning. Tradition is not a disparate collection of extrascriptural truths which the Church has preserved from the Apostles, but rather the whole of Christian truth received, taught, and passed down in the Catholic Church. Tradition preceded Scripture; it was out of tradition that Scripture was formed. Throughout the centuries tradition is the guide

43

which accompanies the Scripture. Tradition gives the key of understanding to those who read the word of God. There is a tradition, there is a Scripture, but the two are one; in indissoluble unity, they are "the basic charter and the life always on the march." Christian truth is found neither in tradition nor in Scripture but in the two linked inseparably.[80]

It should now be more evident why many theologians see the denial of constitutive tradition as a significant step forward in the proper understanding of the Church and revelation. The simplicity of this viewpoint brings into a striking and powerful unity the different organs of the Mystical Body. The Christian revelation contained in the Scriptures is lived by the faithful, expressed in the liturgy, justified and criticized by theologians, directed and led by the hierarchy.[81] Each member has its role to play in the unfolding of doctrine, and only through such a structure can the development of dogma be adequately understood and explained. The whole Church bears the word sacramentally, and it is the word of God lived in the Church and watched over by the magisterium that constitutes the infallible tradition of the Church.[82]

The preceding discussion would indicate, then, that far from being an innovation, this theory is truly traditional; the two-source theory was the innovation. By reaffirming the one-source theory, that is, that the Gospel is transmitted integrally by Scripture and tradition, we re-establish the organic view of the Church held in earlier times. No problem can arise concerning Scripture versus tradition because both are embraced in the unity of the Church. No other doctrine of sources can adequately explain the development of the Church's dogma. In this indissoluble unity of Scripture, Church, and tradition, the existence of constitutive tradition becomes unnecessary and useless. This, at least, is the opinion of many theologians today—but certainly not all. The opinions and evidence of those who dispute this view will be considered next. Let us turn to those who maintain the necessary existence of a constitutive tradition.

Chapter 3

The Affirmative View

THE two preceding chapters have been devoted largely to an exposition of the evidence *against* an extrascriptural and constitutive tradition. This has been necessary because the supposition that all revelation is somehow contained in Scripture sounds strange to most Catholics. Despite the fact that a number of prominent theologians can be cited in support of this theory, the majority of Catholics would no doubt agree with this answer to Protestantism:

"Nothing is found in tradition which is not also found beforehand in the New Testament." Such is not our belief. Such was not the faith of Irenaeus, of Cyprian, of Optatus, of Augustine, nor of any of the ancient Fathers. Tradition can never contradict Scripture but it can very well complete it. It is nowhere stated that Scripture includes everything. It is not through the Scripture, once again, that Jesus Christ decided to transmit His integral message to us.[83]

Many theologians—some to be cited in this chapter—think that it would be highly imprudent to deny the existence of a constitutive tradition. They believe that it is the ecumenical movement that has brought this theory into such prominence at the present time. And it is striking that a large part of the discussion has taken place in ecumenical journals and that the strongest denial of constitutive tradition has been made by theologians particularly interested in the ecumenical movement. However, it is not difficult to see why the question of extrascriptural and constitutive tradition always arises in any ecumenical discussion.[84] If Catholic and Protestant cannot agree on what the Christian revelation is and where it is to be found, then there is not much hope for agreement on many subsequent points. However, if the Catholic theologian can agree with the Protestant that Scripture contains the whole revelation, it would give a new starting point to ecumenical discussions.[85] This would be all the more true since much of present-day Protestantism accepts some concept of tradition, that is, tradition not as a body of extrascriptural truths but as the living and continuing interpretation of holy Scripture.[86] Because of this change of attitude on the part of both Protestant and Catholic theologians, some writers hold out the hope that the Scripture-tradition relationship is not so markedly different for Catholics and Protestants as was formerly thought.

The theologians whom we are studying in this chapter view this movement and this hope as deceptive and illusory. Those who say that all revelation is in Scripture make it sound as if real progress were being made in the direction of Church unity when in fact there is no such progress.[87] The deep doctrinal differences which separate Catholicism and Protestantism on this point cannot be covered over with the statement that all revelation is contained in Scripture; the definition of the dogma of the Assumption should have revealed the unbridgeable gap that divides Protestant and Catholic on this matter.[88]

Because of the ecumenical movement, then, or for other reasons, many Catholic writers immediately accepted the interpretation of the Council of Trent made by Geiselmann and the subsequent denial of constitutive tradition. Some have quickly concluded that the interpretation of Trent put forward in the previous chapter "has been decisively shown by the historical researches of Professor Geiselmann."[89] However, the opponents of this theory claim that the denial of constitutive tradition, far from being decisive, is not well supported in fact. It is one thing to claim that there were two strong currents of thought on this question at Trent, but it is quite another to prove this from the Acts of the Council.[90] The Acts reveal no such thing; on the contrary, they show that there was almost complete unanimity on the incompleteness of Scripture and the need for oral, apostolic traditions to supplement the Scriptures. A large part of the writing that has appeared in the last five years in defense of constitutive tradition has centered on the Council of Trent. For this reason, I shall deal first and at length with the decree of the Council and then add some other historical and doctrinal considerations.

Geiselmann's interpretation of Trent has met with strong opposition in the last few years. Of those who oppose it, none has been more vehement than Henry Lennerz. In his last published article on this subject, Lennerz asked, "How is it possible to explain that so many theologians have not considered or reflected upon the weakness of Professor Geiselmann's arguments, and that in such an important and basic question they have as with eyes closed simply accepted what he has written?"[91] A study of the Council of Trent, he maintained, cannot bear the weight of the new interpretation which places such importance on the elimination of the original *partim-partim* from the text of the final decree. Many distortions of the evidence have been necessary in order to make it appear that the Council made a radical change in the decree at the last moment. It is necessary to reexamine the Council of Trent from this other viewpoint.

The impression is now often given that many Fathers of the Council did not accept the *partim-partim* formula. Actually, only two of the Fathers are mentioned by name in this connection: Nacchianti, the bishop of Chioggia, and Bonucci, the general of the Servites. Nacchianti has been pictured as an expert theologian, highly praised for his learning both by Cardinal Madruzzo and by Cardinal Masarelli, the secretary of the Council. But while it is true that Masarelli said in his diary that Nacchianti was learned, it was only in order to contrast this with the fact that he was also "of little judgment, foolish, imprudent, and more significant, ungrateful, disloyal, uncivil."[92] It seems that Nacchianti was troublesome to all during the Council, and afterwards, in 1548, he was the subject of an examination by the Inquisition, with the commissioner of the Holy Office being the same Masarelli.[93]

Of Nacchianti's objection to the existence of extrascriptural traditions, Geiselmann has said that one would expect the charge of Protestantism to have been raised, but that "Neither the Acts of the Council nor the diaries breathe a word of such an accusation."[94] That this accusation was not made is true, but it is also true that Nacchianti's objection was met by a barrage of scriptural and patristic texts to prove that he was wrong. As Cervini's letter of February 27 to Cardinal Farnese indicated, Nacchianti's opinion was scandalous and was rejected by all.[95] In the April 5 meeting Nacchianti was reprimanded for his statement that it was *impium* to receive tradition with the same reverence as one has for Scriptures. His problem apparently was in distinguishing disciplinary and dogmatic tradition. When the error which sprang from this confusion was finally corrected, Nacchianti did not oppose the formula which stated that revelation is partly in Scripture and partly in tradition. Therefore, the whole Nacchianti affair, far from weakening the position of those who defend constitutive tradition, is "one of their strongest points of support."[96]

Of the Fathers who supposedly opposed the *partim-partim* formula, then, only one can be quoted as explicitly doing so: Bonucci, the general of the Servite Order. It will be recalled that in the April 1 meeting he stated that "all evangelical truth is written." To this assertion there was no reaction recorded among the other Fathers. If Bonucci's opposition were to have worked a radical change in the decree, it must have made a great impression on the Council. But neither the Acts of the Council nor the correspondence of the legates contains a single word which would indicate that the change in the decree was due to Bonucci's objection. An examination of the letters of the Roman legates shows that they recognized no change of opinion to have taken place on the question of extrascriptural tradition. It is hardly possible that they would not have grasped the fact or would not have informed Rome if they had. Not only does Bonucci's opinion seem to have made no great impression on them, but it was apparently unknown to them.[97]

The next point to be considered is the significance of the change which was actually incorporated into the final draft. The recent interpretation supposes that a major revision was effected by the change in wording, and that if the Council did not reverse itself on the existence of extrascriptural revelation, it at least intentionally refrained from affirming positively that there is a constitutive tradition. But the Council left no such doubts; it made itself quite clear on the question. The modification which replaced the words *partim-partim* with *et* was but one of many slight variations in wording which were to be found in the margin of the returned decree. All these variations had the purpose of expressing with maximum clarity what had been decided on by the majority. It is simply unthinkable that a major change could have been effected at this point—against what the overwhelming majority had voted for—without even so much as a mention of the fact.[98]

There is then no real difference in meaning between the final decree with the words "written books and unwritten traditions" and the first formulation of "partly in written books and partly in unwritten traditions"; it is a mistake for a present-day theologian to read a significant change of mind into the action of the Council. Trent's concern was with opposing the "Scripture alone" theory of the reformers, and this it did by asserting the need for oral traditions to supplement the Scriptures.[99] Furthermore, it must be remembered that the only document which has doctrinal authority is the final decree of Trent as it was promulgated. Our concern ought to be with this decree and the doctrine which Trent intended to teach by it. That teaching is clear from the text itself: "The Council wished to teach and clearly taught that one is obliged to accept apostolic traditions which are '*sine scripto*,' that is, truths revealed by God which are not contained in Holy Scripture,"[100] Lennerz points out an important distinction here between "apostolic traditions" and "unwritten traditions"; Trent speaks of the latter. The Council does not oblige the faithful to accept "apostolic tradition" with Scripture but rather "unwritten traditions" with the written books. Scripture and tradition are not mutually exclusive terms, but written books and unwritten traditions are. Holy Scripture can be considered a part of tradition; these two can be overlapping, and as a matter of fact they are. On the other hand, the "unwritten traditions" of which Trent speaks exclude Scripture, and in the decree they are directly contrasted with Scripture. Thus there is a true, extra-scriptural, constitutive tradition which is needed to complement holy Scripture. The decree makes this plain whether the partly-partly formula is there or not.[101]

Indeed, no one in the sixteenth century seems to have had any difficulty in understanding the Tridentine decree. The Council had defined the existence of extra-scriptural truths which pertain to faith; not the legates of the Council nor the theologians nor anyone else at the time interpreted it differently. G. Rambaldi has recently completed studies on two of the theologians present at the Fourth Session of Trent. Concerning one of these, Andrés de Vega, who published his *Tridentini decreti de justificatione* in 1548, Rambaldi concluded that "According to Vega, there are traditions which although they pertain to faith are not found in Scripture . . . . there is no way left open for affirming that all revelation is contained in holy Scripture."[102]

For the theologians whom we are studying in this chapter, the following conclusions would summarize the Council of Trent's position in this matter.

The Council's express purpose was to oppose and refute the Protestant theory of "Scripture alone." It intended to define the existence of oral tradition, received from Christ or from the direct working of the Holy Spirit, which has come down to us from apostolic times. Though the discussion on the matter was somewhat hampered by a lack of precision in terminology, nevertheless, the Council concerned itself with dogmatic tradition and did define the existence of oral traditions which are divine-apostolic and dogmatic.

Concerning the doctrine of two partial sources of revelation, there was almost perfect unanimity in the Council. When it came to accept the decree—including the partly-partly formula—only Bonucci voiced a *non placet*. In regard to the expression "with equal reverence," several bishops preferred the word "similar" in place of "equal." The final decree, however, states that unwritten traditions are to be received with equal reverence (*pari pietatis affectu*). The unwritten traditions were thus given the very same status as the Scriptures.

Everyone at the Council and all the theologians of the time understood the Council to have taught that there are two sources of revelation, namely, canonical Scriptures and oral traditions, which complete and help to interpret Scripture.

That the Acts of the Council were not known in following ages does not affect the matter. The Acts themselves reveal no change of mind on the part of the Council concerning unwritten traditions; as a matter of fact, all indications are to the contrary. In short, "Professor Lennerz has perhaps shown sufficiently clearly that Geiselmann misinterpreted Trent."[103]

Those who defend constitutive tradition maintain that it has always had a place in Catholic theology. It may have been less clear in early days of the Church, but its position has become more and more explicit since the Middle Ages. The Scriptures themselves give no indication that they are meant to be the whole of revelation. If holy Scripture does anything, it testifies to the contrary: "There are many other things which Jesus did that are not written down in this book . . ." (John 20:30); "Do you not remember that when I was still with you, I used to tell you these things?" (II Thess. 2:5). Certainly, there is no way of showing from a study of Scripture itself that it was so planned as to contain all revealed truth. Revelation first existed in the form of oral traditions, and when the Scriptures were composed this would not have done away with the unwritten traditions; the transmission of Christian origins was never confined to a book but was given over to a living Church. Oral tradition, therefore, would have continued to play its legitimate part alongside the written materials.[104] Eventually, these oral traditions became identified with the life of the Church, and because of its continuity the Church can—as Trent declared—bear witness to apostolic traditions which are not contained in holy Scripture.

The Fathers of the early Church did not treat this question in a theoretical way. There is, however, their practical testimony of accepting, for example, the canonicity of the sacred books without any backing from Scripture and therefore on the basis of tradition alone. When the Fathers do speak of the sufficiency of Scripture, they mean a relative kind of sufficiency. The main doctrines of the faith are contained in Scripture, but only by the enrichment of the Church's traditions can a full knowledge of revelation be gained.

By the Middle Ages the distinction between the two sources had begun to emerge. St. Thomas speaks of the "salutary truths" to be found in Scripture, but he also recognizes that, for example, some of the sacraments cannot be found in Scripture. St. Thomas, it would seem, like the other Scholastic theologians, was hesitant and not decisive on this point. The theologians of that era argued from the texts of holy Scripture, but this was not to deny the possibility of oral traditions which would supplement the Scriptures.[105] In the late Middle Ages the distinction between Scripture and tradition became increasingly clear, so that long before Trent the doctrine of two partial sources of revelation was being taught, and the Council merely ratified this common teaching of the pre-Tridentine theologians.[106] The full development of the doctrines of the Catholic faith made it abundantly clear that Scripture is incomplete and requires a complement in the oral traditions.

Post-Tridentine theology, basing itself on the definition of Trent, has always taught the existence of extrascriptural traditions. Theologians were able to understand the Tridentine decree without the inclusion of the partly-partly formula. For present-day theology to suddenly decide that all of revelation is contained in Scripture would be to charge that Catholic theology has been in error these past four hundred years. Finally, the Vatican Council paid much attenton to questions concerning Scripture, and none of the *postulata* of the Bishops suggested that the question of tradition required clarifying. When they came to tradition they had nothing more to say: word for word, the Tridentine decree was taken over and repeated by the Vatican Council. To the Fathers of the nineteenth-century Council, Trent had made itself sufficiently clear on the matter of tradition; or "were they unaware that Bellarmine had distorted Catholic theology?"[107]

It has already been pointed out in the previous chapter that the denial of constitutive tradition would result in a doctrine of admirable simplicity and unity. The theologians whose viewpoint I have elaborated in this chapter admit that there is an undeniable and attractive simplicity to the theory; but this, they believe, is its weakness. The more closely one looks at this new theory, the more it dissolves into unreality. "The more one thinks of the complete corpus of Catholic doctrine, the more does the restriction of tradition as a source to co-extension with that of Scripture appear to be a mirage."[108]

Those who deny that there is a constitutive tradition assert that Scripture is complete as to the contents of revelation, that is, Scripture is materially complete. According to them, the interpretation of the Church is sufficient for the explication of all the dogmas of the Catholic faith. However, it is difficult to see how this theory can possibly be true because Scripture would seem to be incomplete with respect to many points of doctrine in sacramentology and Mariology, and with regard to canonicity.[109]

Concerning the sacraments, it is sometimes said that essential doctrines are contained in sacred Scripture. And it is true that one can point to the water and the formula of baptism as well as to the bread and wine and the words of the holy eucharist.[110] However, one can hardly say that all the essentials concerning extreme unction, confirmation, and matrimony are found in Scripture. It is not just the liturgical rites and ceremonies surrounding these sacraments that are not found in Scripture but actually the essential structure of the sacraments themselves. Indeed, the existence of seven and only seven distinct sacraments is a doctrine of faith that is known only from tradition.[111]

In regard to Mariology, several doctrines which have been defined in modern times have no more than a hint in holy Scripture. Only by means of her oral traditions can the Church supplement what is in Scripture and come to the definition of such doctrines. Admittedly, the doctrine of the Assumption cannot be traced back by a purely historical method to the Apostles, but the doctrine has even less of a basis in Scripture than it has in tradition. Burkhardt tends to think that in dealing with a doctrine like the Assumption, theological method can throw additional light on the earliest historical documents.[112] Another theologian, referring to the Assumption, says that "the possibility should not be overlooked that it is not, in the more significant sense, an instance of development at all, as being also contained explicitly in apostolic tradition."[113] If the doctrine was known in fourth-century Jerusalem, it is quite possible to suppose that it is of much earlier origin, although we may not be able to document it historically. But if the dogma is not contained in Scripture and the Church has nevertheless defined it, then we must assert that it is in tradition.[114]

The one doctrine which is invariably mentioned by those who hold to the existence and necessity of extrascriptural tradition is the doctrine of canonicity. The Church's knowledge that these seventy-two books are inspired and that they alone belong to the Bible is a supernatural truth which can be known only by divine revelation. Even those who are in favor of the theory that revelation is totally in Scripture are often forced to admit that the fixing of the canon cannot be reconciled with their theory.[115] It is hardly conceivable that there should be texts of Scripture which could serve as a basis for the Church's knowledge of the inspiration and canonicity of each of the sacred books. Despite the ingenious attempts to circumvent the problem, the theory that all revelation is contained in Scripture seems to break down here. "It is obviously impossible to accept in a rigid and quite literal sense the formula that all revelation is in Scripture, since . . . the *veritatis manifestativae revelationis* (the canon and inspiration of Scripture, etc.) . . . are clearly contained in tradition alone.[116]

One would think that the above criticism of the theory that all revelation is contained in Scripture would be conclusive. Those who support the theory, however, admit that while many doctrines may not be in holy Scripture in any clear or apparent form, nevertheless there is in Scripture a starting point—however slight—from which each dogma of the faith can be developed. But if this is what these theologians mean by their theory, it would seem to be a misuse of language to say that Scripture "contains" all revelation. "A foundation is not the house that stands upon it, a hint is not a recognized truth, a 'convenient ground' is not a dogma."[117] Geiselmann quotes approvingly the statement of J. B. Kuhn that "in the early ages of the Church we find no dogmatic formulation for which there is not some premise or starting point in Scripture,"[118] and uses this fact as evidence to support his theory that all of revelation is contained in holy Scripture. However, the question raised in opposition to Geiselmann is whether this is what we are to understand by a source or font of revelation. "This is surely a new concept of *fons* and an unwelcome one . . . . The concept of *fons revelationis* has to be inflated to lose much of its value."[119] It is true that the Church in her doctrinal definitions has referred to the Scriptures as an ultimate foundation, but the Church has not said that all doctrines are *contained* in Scripture; indeed, this wording would seem to imply the opposite conclusion.[120]

If, then, one speaks of holy Scripture as sufficient or complete, he must be speaking in a less than literal sense. He is forced to admit that the Scripture is only "relatively complete" and does need to be completed by tradition. If Church, Scripture, and tradition together form an indivisible whole, then Scripture by itself does not contain the whole of revelation.

To summarize; they who defend the existence and the necessity of a constitutive tradition would conclude that revelation, which closed the death of the last Apostle, was handed down to the postapostolic Church in both oral and written forms.[121] The essentials of apostolic tradition, the central mysteries, were consigned to writing. It is not necessary to separate Scripture and tradition, but tradition goes beyond Scripture in both clarity and content.[122]

There is no indication in holy Scripture that this collection of sacred books contains the whole of revelation; the only statements in Scripture are to the contrary. Any supposed plan of the Holy Spirit to make the Scriptures complete cannot be deduced from Scripture itself.[123] There is no *a priori* reason for denying and there is very good reason for accepting the fact that revelation overflowed the language of the Scriptures. It is highly improbable that the revelations arising from personal contact with the Son of God could have been totally recorded in the written word.[124]

The Council of Trent has defined that revelation is contained in "written books and unwritten traditions." The Council Fathers were almost unanimous in the belief that there are unwritten, dogmatic, apostolic traditons which must be accepted in addition to the Scriptures. Post-Tridentine theology has consistently taught the existence of two partial sources of revelation: Scripture and tradition. A denial of this consensus of teaching would require solid proof; no such proof has been brought forward to justify the theory that the contents of Scripture and tradition are identical. Furthermore, the Church has shown no indication in her official teachng of substituting the one-source theory for the two-source theory.

It would seem, then, that this new theory of "totally in Scripture, totally in tradition" must be rejected as unsupported, unjustified, and unapproved.

Chapter 4

The Negative View Reaffirmed

It is apparent in the light of the preceding chapter that the theory which holds revelation to be "totally in Scripture, totally in tradition" has met with some strong opposition. This has increased in the past few years as the work of Geiselmann and others has become more widely known.[125] As might be expected, adherents to this theory have replied to these objections, although it is impossible here to cite specific answers to all the most recent charges. Instead, I will present an outline of that defense, that is, a reaffirmation of the position stated in Chapter 2 as it has been developed or modified in the light of the criticisms discussed in Chapter 3.

The point which has occupied the center of the controversy and about which there seems to be the greatest disagreement is the decree of the Council of Trent. The line of criticism taken by most of the writers referred to in Chapter 3 is that Geiselmann's interpretation is not historically accurate, and the arguments have swirled particularly around the significance of the *partim-partim* text. Chief among these objectors has been Henry Lennerz, long a student of the Council of Trent, whose arguments I have already presented. Now I should like to return once more to the Council of Trent and consider how other theologians have interpreted and answered his criticism.

In one of his studies on this question, Lennerz asks several times, "How can the Council accept apostolic traditions of whose existence the Council is not sure?"[126] There can be only one answer to this question. It was the Council's express purpose to define the existence of *traditiones apostolorum* in opposition to the "Scripture alone" theory of the reformers. There was no doubt in the mind of the Council, nor was there any doubt left in Catholic theology, on the existence of oral, unwritten traditions. But while most of Lennerz's arguments have been toward proving this point, other theologians insist that this is not the real point which needs proving to justify the necessity of constitutive tradition and the so-called two-source theory; the real question is whether Trent defined that there are two *sources* of revelation.

The conclusion Lennerz drew from his question quoted above is that Trent defined the existence of two sources of revelation. However, Trent, as a matter of fact, did not speak of two sources but only one: the source of all saving truth is the Gospel delivered to the Apostles.[127] This point is of capital importance in understanding the decree and in answering the objections of those who assert that Trent has obviously approved of two sources, namely, written books and unwritten traditions. Actually, the Council called neither the written books nor the unwritten traditions a source of revelation; the apostolic preaching of the *Evangelium* is what Trent calls the *fons* of revelation. The canonical books and oral traditions were for Trent the manifestations of revelation through which future ages would come into contact with revealed truth. Furthermore, the preservation of revelation was committed neither to a written text nor to oral tradition but to a living Church. Under the guardianship of the Church, this one truth (*hanc veritatem*) can come to us by either the written or the spoken word.[128]

The previous paragraph would seem to render much less important the insistence of Lennerz on the exclusive character of written and unwritten: "Something cannot be 'written,' that is, found in Scripture, and at the same time be 'unwritten,' that is, not found in Scripture. These terms are exclusive: either written or not written."[129] While it is true that *scriptum* and *non scriptum* are mutually exclusive terms, it is also true that neither *scriptum* nor *non scriptum* constitutes the revelation. They are the channels, reflections, or manifestations of the one revelation, and as a result there can be an overlapping of the truths contained in these two terms.[130] A word cannot be a written word and an unwritten word at the same time, but there is no reason at all why a truth cannot be expressed in both a written and an unwritten form. Whether the truths transmitted in oral tradition are also transmitted through the written text is the point which is *debated;* that it is possible for truths to be transmitted in both ways is *indisputable*. What Trent defined is that there are two channels transmitting revelation from one source. From a purely logical, textual, and *a priori* view, it is impossible to say whether the truths in these two channels coincide in part, are completely identical, or completely exclude one another. Lennerz's rigorous textual arguments, then, do not seem to prove the point that he is intent on proving. Discussion beyond the textual level is both possible and necessary for deciding whether there are truths in the channel of oral tradition that are not at all implied in the written books.

Chapters 2 and 3 have shown that in regard to the *partim-*

partim elimination, Geiselmann has placed great stress on the significance of that change, while those who oppose this interpretation have charged that he is reading his own theory into an historical fact of very slight importance. It would appear that at present some of those who deny the existence of constitutive tradition are willing to grant cogency to Lennerz's evidence on this point. They are willing to admit that Geiselmann's theory cannot be proved from the text itself and that there are no written documents which positively support his interpretation of the *partim-partim* omission. Furthermore, the written proceedings, the letters of the legates, and the interpretation of the theologians of the day do not indicate that a last-minute change or concession was made on account of a minority opposition. They are thus willing to grant that the Council Fathers saw no essential difference between the two formulas. [131] The point they now raise, however, is whether this would destroy their position with regard to Trent. Congar grants that "in the conscious intention of the Fathers, substituting a simple *et* for *partim* had no special significance," but he goes on to add that their action could still have the effect of leaving the question open to further clarification in a later era. "The full human reality of the Councils does not prevent the accomplishment of the intention of a transcendent government."[132]

The Council Fathers did as a matter of fact make a change in the text which seems to express better the relationship of the contents of Scripture and tradition. The first text would at least have given the impression that revelation is divided between two parallel sources; the wording of the final decree is simply noncommittal on the question of their relationship. It is not necessary to insist that the Fathers had in mind what contemporary theology is interested in, namely, whether the truths of tradition are in some way implicit in Scriptures.[133] Without necessarily giving up Geiselmann's interpretation, the point to be insisted upon in this chapter is that there is more to the controversy than the single issue. The denial of a Tridentine decision on constitutive tradition does not necessarily stand or fall with Geiselmann's *partim-partim* interpretation.

From this discussion it is possible to draw some conclusions on the interpretation of the Tridentine decree as it was finally promulgated.

The Council of Trent made no effort to exhaust the question of tradition. As is common with a general council, it defended and defined those points which were under attack at that time. At the very least, it can be said that the nature of tradition is still open to discussion.

The Council emphasized the unity of the Gospel as stemming from the Apostles and being preserved in the continuous life of the Church. The revelation is made known to us through the two-fold instrument of written books and unwritten traditions.

In whatever way one interprets the *partim-partim* omission, it seems that from an historical and logical viewpoint it cannot be shown that the decree of Trent in itself answers the question of whether there are truths contained in oral tradition which are in no way contained in holy Scripture. The arguments raised by Lennerz and others are plausible in many respects, but they do not prove that the truths transmitted orally are in no way reflected in Scripture. After surveying all these opinions concerning Trent, Lengsfeld "cautiously concludes" that Trent did not define the existence of a constitutive tradition, and that it is possible to understand the decree of Trent in a way that is different from the sense in which post-Tridentine thought developed it.[134]

As far as the periods preceding Trent are concerned, it would seem that the matter cannot be decisively settled one way or the other. We have indicated already that it can be misleading to give quotations from patristic or medieval periods to prove the existence or nonexistence of constitutive tradition; the question had not been explicitly formulated or dealt with in the early ages of the Church. However, a study and interpretation of the Fathers and Scholastics would seem to indicate that the more unified picture of Scripture and tradition in those times is, if not a proof of the "totally in Scripture, totally in tradition" theory, in no way incompatible with it. Whereas pre-Tridentine quotations can be found which refer to extrascriptural traditions, we must carefully distinguish references to dogmatic and disciplinary traditions, a distinction not always immediately evident in that era.[135] Furthermore, the belief that all necessary, saving truth is somehow contained in Scripture is a long-standing tradition which did not cease even in the sixteenth century.[136]

With respect to post-Tridentine theology, it must be admitted that Scripture and tradition have generally been treated as if they were separate sources, whether this was an intentional thesis or not. The form of the theology manual, the proof-text approach to the Bible and patristics, and the emphasis on the juridical aspects of the Church have all contributed to the impression that tradition is a stream running parallel to Scripture. This impression, however, is not necessarily a true picture of the matter, and there have been continuing attempts, especially since the nineteenth century, to reunify these sources. It would be shortsighted indeed to think that the ecumenical movement of the past ten years is the only or chief reason for the theory of one unified source. The theory has emerged—or rather re-emerged—over a long period of time coincident with the attempt to better understand the nature of faith, the Mystical Body, and revelation.

Finally, the Church has not decided for or against this theory. The most authoritative and explicit statement of the magisterium is still that of Trent. Vatican I did not reopen the question but merely repeated what Trent had said on it. Neither can the practice of the Church be used as an argument against the theory. On the contrary, the use of Scripture and tradition together, the consistent return to Scripture as a starting point for doctrinal decrees, and the emphasis on the living Church as the proximate norm of faith would seem to be, if not an approval of the presently proposed theory, not opposed to it in any way.

It would therefore appear that no historical facts have been brought to light which would necessitate a radical change in the conclusions of Chapter 2. The history of tradition cannot definitely prove the theory of "totally in Scripture, totally in tradition," but we have seen that the theory is based upon a firm and a long tradition. Though there may have been divisions, the ideal in the history of the Church has always been the perfect unity of Bible, Church, and tradition.

In Chapter 3, the objection was raised that the theory of "totally in Scripture, totally in tradition" is demonstrably false because there are many dogmas of the Church which are not "contained" in Scripture. The doctrines which are nearly always mentioned in this connection are related to canonicity, Mariology, and sacramentology. It would be impossible to try to demonstrate here how particular dogmas in each of these areas are found in Scripture. However, I can indicate some general norms for answering the question. I shall deal first with the problem of canonicity and then take up the larger problem of dogmatic development.

The reason for treating the question of canonicity apart from the rest of the problem may not at first be apparent, but it is necessary to consider canonicity as a unique case before proposing an explanation of the development of doctrine. Because canonicity is a problem that cannot be easily reconciled with a "sufficiency of Scripture" theory, the tendency has been to generalize from this one fact to a stream of constitutive tradition. Canonicity, on the contrary, is not one of the truths in constitutive tradition, but is itself a unique fact. One must admit, too, that it is a uniquely difficult problem to solve; but this would seem to be true whether or not a constitutive tradition is supposed.

It is often said that knowledge of the inspiration of each sacred book must certainly be one fact that has come down in a tradition parallel to Scripture. But those who suppose an explicit oral tradition going back to an Apostle fail to realize that this supposition lacks all historical probability; it does not account for the time and the manner in which the Church gradually came to recognize certain books as inspired.[137] A number of theologians would be quite willing to admit with Bea that while we know that the knowledge of the inspiration of the biblical books is a revealed fact, "How and to whom this revelation was made, we simply do not know."[138]

Many theologians today think that the solution to this problem, at least insofar as it can be solved, lies in a different direction from the assumption of an explicit oral tradition handed down from the Apostles. If the Scriptures were "the primal objectivity of the Church's consciousness," then a separate testimony would seem to be unnecessary for the Church to recognize which books were her own.[139] The Church appears to have decided which books were inspired on the basis of two criteria, apostolicity of origin and agreement with her teaching, working on the normative principle that every apostolic writing willed by God as a constitutive element in the formation of the Church was an inspired book.[140] This fact does not solve all the problems concerning canonicity;[141] nevertheless, approaching the question in this way would seem to be more fruitful than supposing an explicit oral tradition. It seems better to suppose that the fixing of the scriptural canon required an infallible magisterium but not a separate oral testimony traceable to an Apostle. My purpose here is merely to indicate that the fact of canonicity is not necesarrily a part of an extrascriptural and constitutive tradition.

In regard to doctrines like those on the sacraments and Mariology which do not seem to have a clear basis in Scripture, the tendency has been to suppose—as in Chapter 3—that an oral tradition paralleling Scripture is needed to explain the divine revelation of these doctrines. Even where there is no historically verifiable oral tradition, it is assumed that such a tradition does exist and must exist. The thinking of many theologians in recent times, however, is that a good theory of doctrinal development is needed to explain these dogmas, and that such a theory would deliver us from the supposition of an oral—that is, a constitutive —tradition. In one form or another, it must be recognized that a development of considerable proportions has taken place. "Theologians of an earlier day sometimes thought of doctrines of the faith as explicitly held from Apostolic times which had in fact remained implicit till much later. The progress of scientific history has made clearer that there is an organic development of the doctrine in the Church."[142]

God's full revelation to man was made not in words but in the person of Christ. The Gospel transmitted to the Apostles— "the source of all saving truth"—was first of all a living experience. The process of conceptualizing and interpreting revelation began with the Apostles themselves, who had to translate this living experience into formulas for the use of the faithful.[143] The conceptualization into human terms can never be fully adequate, and of itself demands a constant attempt to penetrate its meaning more deeply. This progressive understanding and development of the doctrine of the Church has continued throughout the life of the Church. "The Church derives her life from her own beginnings. . . . It is, however, of the essence of this beginning that it not also be the end."[144]

The question, then, seems to be not whether a development of dogma has taken place but rather how such a development is possible and how the Church proceeds in expounding revelation. To answer these questions we must consider in what sense revelation is "contained" in Scripture and what means the Church uses in interpreting and developing her doctrine.

Those who defend the sufficiency of Scripture maintain that all revelation is contained at least implicitly in Scripture. For many doctrines—an example is the Assumption—there may be only an inkling or a starting point in Scripture, but this is enough to guarantee that all revelation is somehow "contained" in Scripture. Those who dispute this theory assert that it is a semantic exaggeration to say that a doctrine is contained in Scripture when all that is really there is a starting point, a hint, or a suggestion. There may well be a problem of words here; but the verbal difficulty seems to reveal a deeper difference in regard to the very nature of revelation itself and the process by which the Church comes to understand revelation.

Divine revelation consists neither in words nor in propositions but in the realities made known by God. The belief that Scripture is insufficient, that Scripture is only a part of revelation, arises when the mistake is made of too closely identifying the words of the written text with the revelation itself. When revelation is considered to be the stating of a definite number of propositions, then what is not actually stated in the text—or logically deducible from the propositions it contains—is thought to be not "in Scripture" at all.[145]

Revealed truth is "the object of a formal testimony of God"; revelation includes all of that to which God has formally testified.[146] This means that revelation extends to whatever God has intended to communicate, because the content of testimony depends upon what the testifier wishes to convey. A careful distinction must be made between what is communicated and what is stated: What is formally communicated may not be formally stated. What is communicated by a statement goes beyond the stated word, even in human speech; how much more so is this true of the *locutio Dei*. The knowledge of the person speaking, the circumstances of a statement, the tone of voice, and innumerable other elements help communicate the meaning of a statement. Words are the means by which testimony is given, but the context of the words communicates much more than a linguistic analysis of the text would indicate.[147]

This distinction between testimony and statement is of no minor importance in understanding the assertion that revelation is totally in Scripture. Those who say this obviously do not mean that all dogmas are *stated* in Scripture, even implicitly; what they do mean is that all of Catholic dogma is within what is *testified to* or *communicated by* the Scriptures. The statement of Scripture is a window through which the Church looks in order to see what God has intended to communicate to man.[148] The ability to do this is what is guaranteed to the Church in her divine mission. Her reflection is not so much on the words of the text as on the reality communicated by the scriptural witness which is borne by the Church sacramentally.[149] In this light, it is not surprising to find that the Church draws more from Scripture than what the laws of formal logic would entail.

For many years the approach to the question of doctrinal development centered on the definability of the theological conclusion. It is not necessary to enter that debate here since the ideas and terminology used above allow a different approach to the question. Whether, for example, the virtually implicit is sometimes or always part of revelation is not directly relevant to the present remarks.[150] The significant point here is that history indicates that the Church has drawn conclusions from revealed truths and has not in all cases proceeded by the laws of formal logic but rather by some kind of "intuitive insight into the divine purposes and action."[151] At times, this process may even begin with the consensus of belief of the infallible Church and work backwards, as it were, to the necessity of the doctrine in revelation.[152] That the development of dogma is not bound to the laws of syntax and syllogism should be understandable from what has been said about the limits of testimony and the fact that more can be communicated by a statement than the words by themselves would signify. This in turn makes it possible to assert that all revelation is contained in Scripture, that is, that the starting point for the Church's reflection is in Scripture. It is no semantic exaggeration to say that dogma is contained in the Scriptures, because it is precisely by this starting point in Scripture that the Church actually comes to perceive what God has communicated to man.

The private exegete may not be able to deduce from Scripture a particular dogma of the Church. He may find only an argument of fittingness, or he may not even find that; but this does not necessarily mean that the dogma is not contained in Scripture. "For it was only to the Church as a whole that the promise was made that she should possess the original faith entire and unclouded. She alone, and not every isolated individual, has the organs which without fear of error can bring this reflection to completion with universally binding authority."[153] That which was received by the Apostles and expressed in the Scriptures is lived, continued, and developed in the faith of the Church.[154] With this perspective, the notion of a parallel oral tradition to supply truths not adverted to in Scripture becomes both unnecessary and useless. Scripture suggests what the Church authoritatively rules upon. The Church alone can make the decision on whether such a suggested truth is part of the formal testimony of God.

A more fruitful approach to revelation than listing doctrines supposedly absent from Scripture is reading the Scriptures in the light of the Church's understanding.[155] The sufficiency of Scripture makes the development of dogma more intelligible while conferring new meaning on the Bible. "The sufficiency of the Bible is a living protest against its mummification and reduction to a dead letter."[156]

We may conclude therefore, that the doctrinal objections raised in Chapter 3 do not force us to abandon the theory of "totally in Scripture, totally in tradition." While it is no doubt difficult at times to grasp how a doctrine is actually contained in the revelation of the apostolic tradition, "It will be impossible to quote examples in which this reference to early tradition would succeed better by substituting the oral tradition for the Scriptures."[157] Furthermore, what has been said of doctrinal development merely emphasizes the necessity of viewing the Church and Scripture in a reciprocal relationship in which the Bible contains the whole word of God and the Church's tradition proclaims that word with greater penetration and development throughout the centuries.[158]

Chapter 5

The Two Views Compared

BOTH sides of the debate over constitutive tradition have now been set forth, and from all appearances the two positions are diametrically opposed; one asserts that there is a constitutive tradition, the other denies it. Nevertheless, in this concluding chapter I would like to compare the two positions to show not where they differ but where they agree and how the two might be brought more closely together. It would be futile to deny that there really are basic differences of opinion on this matter, but one should not overlook the fact that there are also many points of essential agreement. A different emphasis in certain areas and a clarification of terminology will bring out this underlying unity more fully.

I have dealt with Trent's decree at some length in the three preceding chapters so that there is little to add now to that discussion. There is fundamental disagreement over Geiselmann's theory on the *partim-partim* elimination, and there seems to be little hope that new evidence on that specific point will decide the question one way or the other. But as I pointed out in Chapter 4, perhaps the *partim-partim* problem is being considered in too narrow a context and a broader view of the whole sixteenth-century milieu is necessary for a better understanding of Trent's decree on tradition. An analysis of the vocabulary of both pre-

Tridentine and post-Tridentine writing may be a means to further progress.

With regard to Geiselmann's interpretation, he himself has not claimed that Trent offers proof of his own theory. His main contention is that the Fathers of the Council, with more or less conscious realization of the importance of the matter, left the question open to discussion. Some theologians who have written after Geiselmann have gone beyond him and supposed that Trent had the point which is being argued today explicitly in mind. Their attempts to find positive proof in the Council of Trent for their theory may only tend to confuse the issue and lead the debate away from the main point.

Others whom I mentioned in Chapter 4, among them Beumer, Congar, and Lengsfeld, think that one does not even have to go as far as Geiselmann in order to suppose that the question was left open by Trent; they think that this supposition does not rest solely on the *partim-partim* elimination. This trend of thought may have the value of widening the discussion to a fuller analysis of Tridentine ideas on apostolic and ecclesiastical tradition, the concept of font of revelation, and the idea of faith and morals.

One of the notions that seems to be at the root of much misunderstanding is the use of the word *source*. The theory defending the existence of constitutive tradition is often called the two-source theory as I have said. Those on the opposite side speak of defending "one unified source" of revelation. There is an ambiguity in the word *source* that does not always seem to be recognized. Compare for example; these two statement:

There is then but a single source of revelation, tradition, of which Scripture is the privileged moment and monument.[159]

We think rather . . . that the Council of Trent's decree affirms the existence of two sources. . . .[160]

If one were to assume that these two statements are necessarily opposed to one another, he would be wrong. If one were to think that the second writer is an advocate of the two-source theory he would be even further from the truth. The second writer has said that Trent defined the existence of two sources of revelation, but he is using the word *source* in a different and wider sense than the first writer. The second writer goes on to point out that Trent did not define the relationship of Scripture and tradition, that Trent did not say whether there are truths in oral tradition which are not in Scripture. He maintains, in other words, that Trent did not define the existence of constitutive tradition and so did *not* approve the two-source theory.

The word *source* in this problem can be used in two quite distinct ways. The Gospel which was delivered to the Apostles can be referred to as the source, the font of all revelation. On the other hand, one can also refer to the places where man finds revelation as "sources." In this second usage the emphasis is placed upon our knowledge of revelation, the mode of transmission of revelation, and the work of the theologian. Both of these uses of the word *source* may be defensible, but the two possible meanings ought to be clearly recognized and separated in any debate over the one-source theory versus the two-source theory.[161]

The more restricted and technical use of the word *source* would seem to be the first: the apostolic tradition is the one source of revelation. This is the sense in which Trent used the word. On the other hand, the word *source* is commonly used in the second sense even by writers denying that there is any extrascriptural revelation. It would seem better to use the word in the Tridentine sense, that is, in reference to the revelation delivered to the Apostles in the primitive Church. Some other word— for example, *channel, manifestation, place*—could be used when designating the written books and the unwritten traditions wherein one finds divine revelation. Whether or not there is a constitutive tradition, this distinction of terms is a necessary one and it ought to be acceptable to both sides. To say that there is *one source* (the apostolic tradition) and *two manifestations* (written books and unwritten traditions) is not to decide for or against constitutive tradition. Both sides could accept this distinction and in doing so this would reveal an important area of agreement while also clarifying what the real difference of opinion is.[162]

This ambiguity in the use of the word *source* may indicate that the disagreement is not so wide as might be assumed when one side says, "All revelation is contained in Scripture," and the other side says, "All revelation is not contained in Scripture." It may be found that the statements are not really contradictories because they are not referring to the same thing. Before drawing any conclusions on what the real difference of opinion is, it will be best to summarize what is agreed upon.

First, both sides agree that the whole of revelation is contained in the apostolic tradition, the Gospel, which was delivered to the Apostles by Our Lord and by the inspiration of the Holy Spirit. Second, both sides agree that Scripture is the written form of apostolic tradition in which the essentials of the apostolic message are borne witness to. Scripture is the book in which the Church consigned to writing the central mysteries of Christianity.[163] Third, both agree that revelation, being a living experience, overflows the text of the Bible. What the Apostles experienced could not possibly be fully contained in written propositions.[164] Fourth, both sides agree that there is a tradition and that this tradition "completes" Scripture. Without tradition, God's revelation could not be known even in essentials. A living Church—with oral tradition—is thus necessary.[165] Fifth, both agree that this tradition is truly apostolic, one which can be traced to the primitive Church. It was not a mere text which the Apostles handed down to their successors. The Church, in one way or another, has provided insights into revelation from the beginning of her existence up until our own day.[166] Sixth, both agree that the tradition is something which is closely identified with the life of the Church. Through the help of tradition the Church achieves a deeper knowledge of what is in Scripture. And neither side would subscribe to the theory of a secret gnosis in the early Church, to a body of truths flowing in a stream completely separate from Scripture.[167]

It must be admitted, of course, that the two sides would interpret these statements differently. Nevertheless, the fact that such statements could be acceptable to both reveals a large area of agreement often overlooked. The disagreement, as we have seen, arises over the question of the "sufficiency of Scripture."

The statement is made by those who deny the need for constitutive tradition that all revelation is somehow contained in Scripture. Those who insist on the need for constitutive tradition claim that all revelation is not contained in Scripture. Thus, one says that Scripture is "sufficient" or materially complete; the other side says that Scripture is "insufficient" and incomplete. On the surface, there is a direct contradiction. But from what I have said on the areas of agreement, it would follow that both admit that all dogma is not contained in Scripture in any obvious sense; both admit—or could admit—that Scripture contains a starting point for each dogma;[168] both admit that tradition completes the scriptural hint or suggestion;[169] both admit that tradition is part of the life of the Church stemming from the Apostles. The contradiction, therefore, would seem to be far from perfect.

If both sides say that the starting point in Scripture must be completed by tradition, that it is for the Church to decide whether the suggested truth is part of revelation, where does the real difference of opinion lie? It would seem to come down to this: in what the Apostles passed on to their successors in the Church besides Scripture, was there, in addition to the concrete forms of the Church's life, anything which would at that time have made some of the doctrines suggested in Scripture more explicit? In other words, the main question which divides the two sides is simply to what degree and in what manner the Church develops her dogma.

In the first chapter of this book, the question was asked: is there a constitutive tradition? I remarked that the answer could only be either yes or no. On the basis of that absolute division, Chapters 2, 3, and 4 were composed. Perhaps in conclusion, however, the question may be raised of whether such a debate is soluble in the terms in which it has usually been proposed. The question of a constitutive tradition is certainly a legitimate one; but it is doubtful whether the question will be satisfactorily answered by a direct approach to and an isolated treatment of the problem. There seems to be an amazing amount of misunderstanding on this question, and the misunderstanding is often only heightened by the way the problem is usually discussed.

In a 1961 study, Johannes von Beumer suggests that there is a middle ground between the allegations of the sufficiency and the insufficiency of Scripture.[170] His answer to the problem seems to be not so much a new answer as a reconsideration of the problem and a restatement of the answer in terms more acceptable to both sides.[171] He accomplishes this by concentrating his attention primarily on the unity of Scripture and tradition. In doing so, he distinguishes his position from that which posits a separate oral tradition which adds new truths to the contents of Scripture, and yet he also stands apart from those who maintain that tradition is the "homogeneous unfolding" of the Scriptures.[172] Beumer maintains that one must begin with the organic unity of Scripture and tradition; both of these gravitate about the same revelation, both cover the same essential ground. Scripture supplies the starting point for each doctrine and tradition goes beyond the Scripture "only in a relatively subordinated degree."[173] In the sense of material completeness, the Scriptures could be called "sufficient," but Beumer prefers not to use the expression and not to phrase the question in those terms. In this view, what holds primacy is the unity of Scripture and tradition. Scripture is complete in the sense in which such a written witness could be complete; tradition is needed to complete Scripture in the sense in which an understanding of the written word is necessary for a living Church.

This approach to the question, through the unity of Church, Scripture, and tradition, would appear to be the most promising and fruitful one. Just as the historical discussion sometimes becomes too narrow in outlook, so also the doctrinal problems which envelop this question are sometimes lost sight of. One must keep in mind the whole process of how God speaks to man through the Church, which is the Body of Christ, and how man comes into contact through faith with God's saving word. There is a Church, there is a tradition, there is a Bible; their interrelationship must be explained. Nothing is more important for the Church today than the harmonious and organic unity of Scripture, Church, and tradition. Some would seem to have rejected out of hand the theory of "totally in Scripture, totally in tradition" without actually considering the whole question. They have rejected not the truth of this theory but the possibility of it, and this would seem to be doing injustice to the great number of theologians in the world today who defend it.

On the other side, it is possible, of course, to deny that all revelation is "contained" in Scripture, but perhaps there is need for more discussion on what is meant by *contained* as used in this sentence. Before an agreement can be reached on whether all revelation is contained in Scripture, some agreement has to be reached on how any revelation is "contained" there. In this connection, there would seem to be little value in arguing that all the dogmas of the Catholic faith cannot be deduced from Scripture; everyone admits that. It may be of value, however, to consider that the Church has not always proceeded by way of deduction. The Church would seem to work with a more than human logic in understanding and interpreting revelation. Theoretically and abstractly, one might conceive of the Church as an institution preserving intact its books containing revelation and its original traditions and at the most drawing some logical conclusions. In actual fact, however, this is not what history reveals. There has been a true progression, a considerable development in the Church's penetration, understanding, and exposition of revelation. At the same time, as the Church moves through space and time, she never leaves aside apostolic testimony, which is her "one source of saving truth." Of this apostolic tradition she has a written record in the Scriptures and an oral testimony which began with the Apostles and has never been discontinued throughout her life. She does not separate the two; it is neither the book nor the oral teaching that transmits revelation but Scripture and tradition linked inseparably in the Church.

Those who deny the existence of constitutive tradition insist that what they are most interested in is the unity of Scripture and tradition, which they believe has been lost in post-Tridentine theology. But perhaps they would progress farther in that direction by stressing the unity of the two rather than the sufficiency of Scripture and nonexistence of constitutive tradition. This is not to deny the "sufficiency of Scripture" in the sense in which these writers use the term, but what is highly doubtful is whether focusing on this point helps clarify the matter. What seems more often to happen is that the argument bogs down in the consideration of whether the Scriptures are "sufficient" or "insufficient." One may wonder if this should be the main point of the discussion when as a matter of fact no one maintains that Scripture is sufficient *apart* from the Church's tradition. To speak of the Scriptures as having material completeness in themselves seems only to confuse the issue; apart from tradition, Scripture does not have completeness—it has no existence at all.

Those who maintain the need for constitutive tradition might also concentrate less on the insufficiencies of Scripture and more on the organic unity of Scripture and tradition. They might do well to consider the attitude of the Church toward Scripture, the whole question of the Church's doctrinal development, and the way in which the Church proceeds in using Scripture and tradition together. If the unity of Scripture and tradition were their chief emphasis also, perhaps they would find their position not so far removed from the opposite theory as it first seemed. With the same starting point in the unity of Scripture and tradition, with charity on both sides, and with the desire of everyone to see all aspects of the question, a progressive clarification of the Scripture-tradition relationship will no doubt be realized.

Many times throughout this work the matter of ecumenical considerations has arisen. Some theologians seem particularly interested in the question we have been discussing because of its significance in the ecumenical movement; other Catholic writers fear that this desire for Christian unity may lead to distortions of Catholic doctrine. Whatever the correct formulation of this particular doctrine is, Pope John XXIII indicated that our part in achieving Christian unity lies with renewal in the Church. Reunion is bound up with the increase of Catholic faith, the renewal of Christian morality, and the adaptation of ecclesiastical discipline.[174] One part of this renewal might be a clearer statement and a more profound realization of how God's word is proclaimed to man. God breaks into human history to speak to man from out of the Church, the continuation of Christ in the world. But the exact manner in which the Church bears God's word to the world may not be entirely clear. The debate we have studied in this book indicates that the time may be close at hand for the Church to further clarify this doctrine. We confidently look forward to the time when the Church will add to Trent's declaration and will state the Catholic doctrine on this matter in terms best suited to our own day.

Bibliography

Adam, Karl, *The Christ of Faith*, tr. Joyce Crick. New York: Pantheon, 1957.

Bacht, Henrich von, *"Tradition und Lehramt in der Diskussion um das Assumpta-Dogma."* In Michael Schmaus, ed., *Die mündliche Überlieferung*. Munich: Hueber, 1957.

——, *"Tradition als menschliches und theologisches Problem."* *Stimmen der Zeit*, CLIX (January, 1957), 285–300.

——, *"Tradition und Sakrament."* *Scholastik*, XXX (January, 1955), 1–32.

Baepler, Richard, "Scripture and Tradition in the Council of Trent." *Concordia Theological Monthly*, XXXI (June, 1960), 341–362.

Baumgartner, Charles, *"Tradition et Magistère."* *Recherches de Science religieuse*, XLI (April, 1953), 161–187.

Benard, Edmond, "A Development of Doctrine: A Basic Framework." *Proceedings: Fifth Annual Meeting, Society of Catholic College Teachers of Sacred Doctrine*, V (1959), 14–29.

Beumer, Johannes von, *"Das katholische Schriftprinzip in der theologischen Literatur der Scholastik bis zur Reformation."* *Scholastik*, XVI (January, 1941), 24–52.

——, *"Das katholische Traditionsprinzip in seiner heute neu erkennten Problematik."* *Scholastik*, XXXVI (April, 1961), 217–240.

——, *"Katholisches und protestantisches Schriftprinzip im Urteil des Trienter Konzils."* *Scholastik*, XXXIV (April, 1959), 249–258.

Bévenot, Maurice, "Faith and Morals in the Council of Trent and Vatican I." *Heythrop Journal*, III (January, 1962), 15–30.

Bévenot, Maurice, review of George Tavard, *Holy Writ or Holy Church.* In *Theological Studies,* XXI (September, 1960), 484–485.

——, "Tradition, Church and Dogma." *Heythrop Journal,* I (January, 1960), 34–47.

Bouyer, Louis, *The Spirit and Forms of Protestantism,* tr. A. V. Littledale. Westminster: Newman, 1957.

Braun, F.-M., *"La Bible dans la Vie de l'Église à la Lumière du Nouveau Testament."* Bible et vie chrétienne, XII (December, 1955), 35–40.

Brinkmann, Bernard, *"Inspiration und Kanonizität der Hl. Schrift in ihrem Verhältnis zur Kirche."* Scholastik. XXXIII (April, 1958), 208–233.

Brown, Robert McAfee, "Tradition as a Protestant Problem." *Theology Today,* XVII (January, 1961), 430–454.

Bulst, Werner, *Offenbarung.* Düsseldorf: Patmos, 1960.

Burke, Eugene, "The Use of Sacred Scripture as a Locus Theologicus." *Proceedings: Fourteenth Annual Convention, Catholic Theological Society of America,* XIV (1960), 54–96.

Burkhardt, Walter, "The Catholic Concept of Tradition in the Light of Modern Theological Thought." *Proceedings: Sixth Annual Convention, Catholic Theological Society of America,* VI (1951), 42–75.

——, "The Mariologist as Ecumenist." *Marian Studies,* XIII (1962), 5–12.

Butler, B. C., *The Church and the Bible.* Baltimore: Helicon, 1960.

Congar, Yves, "Holy Writ and Holy Church." *Blackfriars,* XLI (January, 1960), 11–19.

——, *La Tradition et les Traditions.* Paris: Arthème Fayard, 1960.

——, *"Traditions apostoliques non écrites et Suffisance de l'Écriture."* Istina, VI (July, 1959), 279–306.

Cristiani, Leon, and Jean Rilliet, *Catholics and Protestants.* Westminster: Newman, 1960.

Cullmann, Oscar, *The Early Church*, ed. A. J. B. Higgins. Philadelphia: Westminster, 1956.

———, *La Tradition*. Neuchâtel: Delachaux et Niestlé, 1953.

Daniélou, Jean, *"Écriture et Tradition dans le Dialogue entre les Chrétiens séparés."* *Documentation catholique*, LIV (March, 1957), 283–294.

———, *God and the Ways of Knowing*, tr. Walter Roberts. New York: Meridian, 1957.

Davis, Charles, "The Living Word." *Worship*, XXXII (October, 1958), 518–531.

———, "Mariology." *Clergy Review*, XLIII (April, 1958), 274–294.

Dejaifve, G., *"Bible et Tradition dans le Luthéranisme contemporain."* *Nouvelle Revue théologique*, LXXVIII (January, 1956), 33–49.

———, *"Bible, Tradition, Magistère dans la Théologie catholique."* *Nouvelle Revue théologique*, LXXVIII (February, 1956), 135–151.

Dhanis, Edward, *"Revelation explicite et implicite."* *Gregorianum*, XXXIV (April, 1953), 186–237.

Dillenschneider, Clement, *Le premier Principe d'une Théologie mariale organique*. Paris: Alsatia, 1955.

———, *Le Sens de la Foi et le Progrès dogmatique du Mystère marial*. Paris: Academia Mariana Internationalis, 1954.

Dubarle, A.-M. *"La Bible et les Théologiens."* *Revue des Sciences philosophiques et théologiques*, XXXIX (January, 1955), 72–77.

———, *"Écriture et Tradition à propos de Publications récentes."* *Istina*, IV (January, 1957), 113–128.

———, *"Les Fondements bibliques du titre marial de nouvelle Ève."* *Recherches de Science religieuse*, XXXIX (January, 1951), 49–64.

Egloff, Eugen, *"Die ökumenische Haltung des Katholiken."* In Oscar Cullmann and Otto Karrer, eds., *Einheit in Christus*. Zurich: Benziger, 1960.

Ehrlich, R., "Papacy and Scripture." *Scottish Theological Journal*, XV (June, 1962), 113–123.

Extremeño, C. G., *"El Sentido de la Fe, Criterio de la Tradición."* *Ciencia Tomista*, LXXXVII (July, 1960), 569–606.

Fannon, Patrick, "The Protestant Approach to Mariology." *Irish Theological Quarterly*, XXIX (April, 1962), 121–135.

Geenen, G., "The Place of Tradition in the Theology of Saint Thomas." *Thomist*, XV (January, 1952), 110–135.

Geiselmann, Josef, *"Das Konzil von Trient über das Verhältnis der Heiligen Schrift und der nicht geschrieben Traditionen."* In Michael Schmaus, ed., *Die mündliche Überlieferung*. Munich: Hueber, 1957.

——, *"Un Malentendu éclairci: La Relation 'Écriture-Tradition' dans la Théologie catholique."* *Istina*, V (April, 1958), 197–214.

——, "Scripture, Tradition, and the Church: An Ecumenical Problem." In Daniel Callahan, Heiko Oberman, and Daniel O'Hanlon, eds., *Christianity Divided*. New York: Sheed and Ward, 1961.

——, *"Die Tradition."* In J. Feiner, J. Trütsch, and F. Böckle, eds., *Fragen der Theologie heute*. Einsiedeln: Benziger, 1958.

Hanson, R., "The Church and Tradition in the Pre-Nicene Fathers." *Scottish Theological Journal*, XII (January, 1959), 21–31.

Henry, A.-M., ed., *Introduction to Theology*, tr. William Story. Theology Library, vol. I; Chicago: Fides, 1954.

Holstein, Henri, *"La Tradition catholique."* *Études*, CCCI (June, 1959), 346–354.

——, *"La Tradition d'après le Concile de Trente."* *Recherches de Science religieuse*, XLVII (July, 1959), 367–390.

——, *La Tradition dans l'Église*. Paris: Grasset, 1960.

Ibañez Arana, Andrés, *"Escritura y Tradición en el Concilio de Trento."* *Lumen*, VII (July, 1958), 336–344.

Iturrioz, Daniel, *"Tradición y Revelación."* *Razon y Fe*, CLXIII (May, 1961), 453–468.

——, *"Tradición y Revelación en el Concilio Vaticano y su Época."* *Estudios Eclesiásticos*, XXXVII (April, 1962), 171–217.

Jasinski, V. J., "Methodological Riddle of 'Munificentissimus Deus.'" *Homiletic and Pastoral Review,* LII (October, 1951), 16–21.

Jedin, Hubert, *A History of the Council of Trent,* tr. Ernest Graf. London: Nelson, 1961, vol. II.

Jenkins, Daniel, *Tradition, Freedom and the Spirit.* Philadelphia: Westminster, 1951.

Jones, Alexander, *God's Living Word.* New York: Sheed and Ward, 1961.

Journet, Charles, *Esquisse du Développement du Dogme marial.* Paris: Alsatia, 1954.

Karrer, Otto, "*Apostolische Nachfolge und Primat.*" In J. Feiner, J. Trütsch, and F. Böckle, eds., *Fragen der Theologie heute.* Einsiedeln: Benziger, 1958.

———, "*Ruckblick und Ausblick.*" In Oscar Cullmann and Otto Karrer, eds., *Einheit in Christus.* Zurich: Benziger, 1960.

Koch, W., "*Der Begriff Traditiones im Trienter Konzildekret der Sessio iv.*" *Theologische Quartalschrift,* CXXXII (January–April, 1952), 46–61, 193–211.

Köster, Heinrich, "Protestant Reaction to Mary's Assumption." *Theology Digest,* V (Spring, 1957), 105–108.

Küng, Hans, *The Council, Reform and Reunion,* tr. Cecily Hastings. New York: Sheed and Ward, 1961.

———, *Rechtfertigung.* Paderborn: Johannes Verlag, 1957.

Latourelle, René, "*Église et Parole.*" *Sciences ecclésiastiques,* XIV (May, 1962), 195–212.

———, "*Notion de Révélation et Magistère de l'Église.*" *Sciences ecclésiastiques,* IX (October, 1957), 201–261.

Lattey, C., review of Alan Richardson and William Schweitzer, *Biblical Authority for Today.* In *Scripture,* V (July, 1952), 79.

Lecler, Joseph, "*Église, Magistère, et Tradition.*" *Recherches de Science religieuse,* XLIX (July, 1961), 442–456.

Leclerq, Jean, *The Love of Learning and the Desire for God*. New York: Fordham University Press, 1961.

Leenhardt, F. J., *"Sola Scriptura, ou: Écriture et Tradition."* *Études théologiques religieuses*, XXXVI (January, 1961), 5–46.

Lennerz, Henry, *"Scriptura Sola."* *Gregorianum*, XL (January, 1959), 38–53.

———, *"Scriptura et Traditio."* *Gregorianum*, XLII (July, 1961), 517–522.

———, *"Sine Scripto Traditiones."* *Gregorianum*, XL (April, 1959), 624–635.

Leonard, A., *"La Foi, principe fondamental du Développement du Dogme."* *Revue des sciences philosophiques et théologiques*, XLII (April, 1958), 276–286.

Lodrioor, Joseph, *"Écriture et Traditions."* *Ephemerides Theologicae Lovanienses*, XXXV (April, 1959), 423–427.

Loewenich, Walter von, *Modern Catholicism*, tr. Reginald Fuller. New York: St. Martin's, 1959.

Mackey, J. P., *The Modern Theology of Tradition*. New York: Herder and Herder, 1963.

Martín, Benjamín, *"La Sagrada Escritura y la Tradición apostólica."* *Cultura Bíblica*, XV (January, 1958), 22–26.

McKenzie, John L., review of Karl Rahner, *Inspiration in the Bible*. In *Theological Studies*, XXIII (March, 1962), 104–106.

Moran, V., *"Scripture and Tradition: A Current Debate."* *Australian Catholic Record*, XXXVIII (January, 1961), 14–22.

Mouson, J., *"De Relatione inter S. Scripturam et Traditionem."* *Collectanea Mechliniensia*, XXX (1960), 138–143.

Murphy, John L., *The Notion of Tradition in John Driedo*. Milwaukee: Seraphic, 1959.

———, *"Unwritten Traditions at Trent."* *American Ecclesiastical Review*, CXLVI (April, 1962), 233–263.

Ortigues, Edmond, "Écriture et Traditions apostoliques au Concile de Trente." Recherches de Science religieuse, XXXVI (April, 1949), 270–299.

Outler, Albert, The Christian Tradition and the Unity We Seek. New York: Oxford, 1957.

Owens, Gerard, "Is All Revelation Contained in Sacred Scripture?" Studia Montis Regii, I (1958), 55–60.

Pelikan, Jaroslav, "Issues That Divide Us: Protestant." In Christians in Conversation. Westminster: Newman, 1962.

———, The Riddle of Roman Catholicism. New York: Abingdon, 1959.

Pozo, Cándido, "La Tradición en la XXI Semana española de Teología." Estudios Eclesiásticos, XXXVII (April, 1962), 219–236.

Rahner, Karl, Inspiration in the Bible, tr. Charles Henkey. New York: Herder & Herder, 1961.

———, Theological Investigations, tr. C. Ernst. Baltimore: Helicon, 1961, vol. I.

Rambaldi, G., "In Libris scriptis et sine scripto traditionibus. La interpretazione del teologo conciliare G. A. Delfino." Antonianum, XXXV (January, 1960), 88–94.

———, "Un Texto del franciscano Andrés de Vega sobre la Tradición." Estudios Eclesiásticos, XXXIII (October, 1959), 429–432.

Ratzinger, Joseph, "Offenbarung, Schrift, Überlieferung." Trierer theologische Zeitschrift, LXVII (January, 1958), 13–27.

Reid, J. K. S., The Authority of Scripture. London: Methuen, 1957.

———, "Roman Catholicism and the Bible." Interpretation, XIII (January, 1959), 71–86.

Rich, Edward, Spiritual Authority in the Church of England. London: Longmans, Green, 1953.

Robert, A., and A. Tricot, Initiation biblique. 3rd ed.; Paris: Desclée, 1954.

St. John, Henry, "The Approach to Unity Through the Scriptures." *Blackfriars*, XLII (October, 1961), 398–405.

———, "The Authority of Doctrinal Development." *Blackfriars*, XXXVI (1955), 372–381, 412–424, 483–493.

———, "Bible and Tradition." *Blackfriars*, XXXIX (August, 1958), 300–309.

———, *Essays in Christian Unity*. Westminster: Newman, 1955.

Salaverri, Joaquim, "*La Tradición valorada como Fuente de la Revelación en el Concilio de Trento.*" *Estudios Eclesiásticos*, XX (January, 1946), 33–61.

Scheffczyk, Leo, "*Biblische und dogmatische Theologie.*" *Trierer theologische Zeitschrift*, LXVII (1958), 193–209.

Schenk, Berthold von, "Factors That Unite Us: Protestant." In *Christians in Conversation*. Westminster: Newman, 1962.

Schmaus, Michael, *Katholische Dogmatik*. Munich: Hueber, 1960, vol. I.

Semmelroth, Otto, "*Die Heilige Schrift als Glaubensquelle.*" *Stimmen der Zeit*, CLXI (January, 1958), 36–50.

Spindeler, A., "*Pari pietatis affectu. Das Tridentinum über Heilige Schrift und apostolische Überlieferung.*" *Theologie und Glaube*, LI (March, 1961), 161–180.

Stanley, David, "Concept of Biblical Inspiration." *Proceedings: Thirteenth Annual Convention, Catholic Theological Society of America*, XIII (1959), 65–96.

Stevenson, Anthony, "The Development and Immutability of Christian Doctrine." *Theological Studies*, XIX (December, 1958), 481–533.

Sweeney, John, "The Challenge to Theology." *Proceedings: Thirteenth Annual Convention, Catholic Theological Society of America*, XIII (1959), 178–191.

Tavard, George, "The Authority of Scripture and Tradition." In John Todd, ed., *Problems of Authority*. Baltimore: Helicon, 1962.

——, "A Forgotten Theology of Inspiration: Nikolaus Ellenbog's Refutation of 'Scriptura Sola.'" *Franciscan Studies,* XV (1955), 106–122.

——, *Holy Writ or Holy Church.* New York: Harper, 1959.

——, "Is Tradition a Problem for Catholics?" *Union Seminary Quarterly Review,* XVI (May, 1961), 375–384.

——, "The Recovery of an Organic Notion of Tradition." *The Liturgy and Unity in Christ,* 21st Liturgical Week, 1960, pp. 122–129.

——, "Scripture, Tradition and History." *Downside Review,* LXXII (1954), 232–244.

——, "Some Remarks on the Liturgy as Tradition." *Worship,* XXVIII (1954), 467–471.

——, "Tradition in Early Post-Tridentine Theology." *Theological Studies,* XXIII (September, 1962), 377–405.

——, "Tradition and Scripture." *Worship,* XXXV (May, 1961), 375–381.

Thurian, Max, *"La Tradition."* *Verbum Caro,* LVII (January, 1961), 49–98.

Turner, Henry E., *The Patterns of Christian Truth.* London: Mowbray, 1954.

Van Noort, G., *The Sources of Revelation: Divine Faith,* tr. and rev. W. R. Murphy and J. J. Castelot, vol. III of *Dogmatic Theology.* Westminster: Newman, 1961.

Vawter, Bruce, *The Bible and the Church.* New York: Sheed and Ward, 1959.

Vollert, Cyril, "Doctrinal Development: A Basic Theory." *Proceedings: Twelfth Annual Convention, Catholic Theological Society of America,* XII (1957), 45–74.

Vooght, Paul de, *"Écriture et Tradition d'après des Études catholiques récentes."* *Istina,* V (April, 1958), 183–196.

Vooght, Paul de, *Les Sources de la Doctrine chrétienne*. Paris: Desclée de Brouwer, 1954.

Weigel, Gustave, "Catholic Ecclesiology in Our Time." In Daniel Callahan, Heiko Oberman, and Daniel O'Hanlon, eds., *Christianity Divided*. New York: Sheed and Ward, 1961.

——, *Catholic Theology in Dialogue*. New York: Harper, 1961.

Notes

[1] We should remark at the beginning that revelation is never really an object which can be divided, contained, or put into categories. The loving invitation of the merciful God revealed in Christ can only be proclaimed to man by the Church and answered by man in faith. If in studying the present question I am forced to use language which tends to objectify that revelation, it should be obvious that the reification of God's word is never intended.

[2] In recent years many books have appeared that deal wholly or in part with the problem under consideration here. The Bibliography at the end of this study gives some indication of that fact. Two histories of tradition have recently been published in French: Yves Congar, *La Tradition et les Traditions* (Paris: Arthème Fayard, 1960) and Henri Holstein, *La Tradition dans l'Église* (Paris: Grasset, 1960). In German, a number of recent works treat of the problem, notably, Peter Lengsfeld, *Überlieferung und Schrift in der evangelischen und katholischen Theologie der Gegenwart* (Paderborn: Bonifacius Druckerei, 1960), and Michael Schmaus, ed., *Die mündliche Überlieferung* (Munich: Hueber, 1957). The ecumenical dialogue in Germany has produced a number of books which deal in part with the question of the Scripture-tradition relationship, for example, M. Roesle and Oscar Cullman, eds., *Begegnung der Christen* (Stuttgart: Evangelischen, 1959), and Oscar Cullmann and Otto Karrer, eds., *Einheit in Christus* (Zurich: Benziger, 1960). Other works, such as J. Feiner, J. Trütsch, and F. Böckle, eds., *Fragen der Theologie heute* (Einsiedeln: Benziger, 1958); J. Betz and H. Fries, eds., *Kirche und Überlieferung* (Freiburg: Herder, 1960); and the new edition of Michael Schmaus, *Katholische Dogmatik* (Munich: Hueber, 1960), vol. I, incorporate some of the more recent conclusions. In English, one of the few full-length treatments is George Tavard, *Holy Writ or Holy Church* (New York: Harper, 1959). A specialized treatment of the pre-tridentine period is John L. Murphy, *The Notion of Tradition in John Driedo* (Milwaukee: Seraphic, 1959). A few other works contain shorter essays on the question,

as, for example, Daniel Callahan, Heiko Oberman, and Daniel O'Hanlon, eds., *Christianity Divided* (New York: Sheed and Ward, 1961), or touch upon the question in passing, as Alexander Jones, *God's Living Word* (New York: Sheed and Ward, 1961); Louis Bouyer, *The Spirit and Forms of Protestantism,* tr. A. V. Littledale (Westminster: Newman, 1957); and Karl Rahner, *Inspiration in the Bible,* tr. Charles Henkey (New York: Herder & Herder, 1961). Even with these and similar titles, however, the number of books on this question is still relatively small, particularly in the English language, where there is nothing comparable, for example, to Lengsfeld's book. It is thus necessary to look to the theological journals in order to see the full development of the problem.

[3] The two best-known German histories of tradition were both published some thirty years ago: August Deneffe, *Der Traditionsbegriff* (Munster: Aschendorffsche, 1931), and Joseph Ranft, *Der Ursprung des katholischen Traditionsprinzip* (Wurzburg: Triltsch, 1931). In recent years, probably the most complete treatment is to be found in Congar's work, which he, however, views as merely a sketch or outline. The work of Tavard which I have cited is a history of tradition up to the Reformation. Other studies of tradition in particular historical periods can be found in journal articles; some of these will be cited in the course of the present study.

[4] Denzinger 783. Translation is from John Clark, *et al., The Church Teaches* (St. Louis: Herder, 1955), p. 45.

[5] G. Van Noort, *The Sources of Revelation: Divine Faith,* tr. and rev. J. J. Castelot and W. R. Murphy, vol. III of *Dogmatic Theology* (Westminster: Newman, 1961), p. 139.

[6] *Ibid.,* p. 146.

[7] This has been particularly so since the time of Franzelin. The heavy emphasis on the close relationship can be seen in a statement such as the following by Henri Holstein: "Although it is not exact to identify the magisterium with tradition, it ought to be realized that the best, the surest, and the most usual witness to the apostolic tradition is the teaching of the Church's hierarchy" (*"La tradition catholique,"* Études, CCCI [June, 1959], 353). Even stronger is Deneffe's statement: "Tradition in the primary sense is the infallible teaching of the faith exercised by the magisterium" (quoted in Charles Baumgartner, *"Tradition et Magistère,"* Recherches de Science religieuse, XLI [April, 1953], 163; this entire article

by Baumgartner is devoted to the necessary distinction between magisterium and tradition).

8 That this terminology is open to confusion is hardly surprising, especially when the word *apostolic* is used alone. More often than not, the word *apostolic* is equated with what is here more precisely designated *divine-apostolic*. As will be pointed out later, one of the chief difficulties in determining the meaning of Trent's discussions is that the concept *apostolic tradition(s)* is not at all clear. For example, in the proposal of the group headed by Del Monte on February 12, 1546 the word *ecclesiastical* is used in the sense in which we would use the word *apostolic*. See Henri Holstein, *"La Tradition d'après le Concile de Trente," Recherches de Science religieuse*, XLVII (July, 1959), 370; compare Murphy, *op. cit.*, p. 63. Even at present, one must be careful of a change of meaning especially when the words are used with reference to Protestant writers. When Daniélou writes, "All that Cullmann says of the authority of the apostolic tradition must be attributed to the ecclesiastical tradition," he is using a different terminology than that proposed here (see Jean Daniélou, *"Écriture et Tradition dans le Dialogue entre les Chrétiens séparés," Documentation catholique*, LIV [March, 1957], 287).

9 Once again, these definitions were not at all clear in earlier ages; particularly in the sixteenth century. Disciplinary and dogmatic traditions were often lumped together when reference was made to apostolic traditions. See John L. Murphy, "Unwritten Traditions at Trent," *American Ecclesiastical Review*, CXLVI (April, 1962), 242–243.

10 What is declarative in the Catholic sense of the word might be constitutive tradition to the Protestants. In Protestant thought, only what is said to be formally contained in Scripture is called declarative. In what way declarative tradition may be contained in Scripture according to Catholic theologians I will discuss later.

11 A possible ambiguity can arise over the word *constitutive*. Deneffe and others use this word to refer to the whole body of truths revealed to the Apostles, as opposed to *continuative* tradition or the preservation of those truths. See Murphy, "Unwritten Traditions at Trent," p. 239. I shall avoid this second meaning of constitutive tradition in the course of this book.

12 In what sense the word *contains* is here used is one of the main points which must be investigated in the following chapters.

[13] A difficulty arises because some have equated constitutive tradition with tradition as such. If this were true, then the denial of constitutive tradition would be a denial of tradition. Generally, Catholic theologians today have a broader idea of tradition, whatever their opinion is concerning the existence of constitutive tradition.

[14] See Walter Burkhardt, "The Catholic Concept of Tradition in the Light of Modern Theological Thought, *Proceedings: Sixth Annual Convention, Catholic Theological Society of America,* VI (1951), 43. Burkhardt quotes an article of Berthold Altaner written in 1950.

[15] See V. J. Jasinski, "Methodological Riddle of 'Munificentissimus Deus,'" *Homiletic and Pastoral Review,* LII (October, 1951), 16–21; Charles Journet, *Esquisse du Développement du Dogme marial* (Paris: Alsatia, 1954), p. 18; G. Filograssi, "*Tradizione Divino-Apostolica e Magistero,*" in *Lo Sviluppo del Dogma* (Rome: Gregorian, 1953), pp. 135–167; and Cyril Vollert: "The definition of the Assumption did not rely either on historical evidence from the first Christian centuries or on theological conclusions" ("Doctrinal Development: A Basic Theory," *Proceedings: Twelfth Annual Convention, Catholic Theological Society of America,* XII [1957], p. 45).

[16] See Rahner, *op. cit.,* p. 75, and Heinrich von Bacht, "*Tradition und Lehramt in der Diskussion um das Assumpta-Dogma,*" in Schmaus, ed., *op. cit.,* pp. 38–62. It is interesting to note that many Mariologists are among those who deny the existence of constitutive tradition; Charles Davis says, "Leading Mariologists today unambiguously affirm that the initial deposit from which all the revealed truths on Our Lady is derived is given in the Bible" ("Mariology," *Clergy Review,* XLIII [April, 1958], 282). See also, for example, A.-M. Dubarle, "*Les Fondements bibliques du titre marial de nouvelle Ève,*" *Recherches de Sciences religieuses,* XXXIX (January, 1951), 50–51; Clement Dillenschneider, *Le premier Principe d'une Théologie mariale organique* (Paris: Alsatia, 1955), pp. 88–93; and Journet, *op. cit.,* p. 40. That this is still an open question among Mariologists, however, is pointed out in the presidential address to the 1962 Mariological Society meeting; see Walter Burkhardt, "The Mariologist as Ecumenist," *Marian Studies,* XIII (1962), 10.

[17] Congar, *op. cit.,* p. 76.

[18] For the effect of modern biblical studies, especially form criticism, on Protestant concepts of tradition, see Daniel Jenkins, *Tradition, Freedom*

and the Spirit (Philadelphia: Westminster, 1951), pp. 17–18; G. Gloege and G. Ebeling as summarized in G. Dejaifve, *"Bible et Tradition dans le Luthéranisme contemporain,"* *Nouvelle Revue théologique,* LXXVIII (January, 1956), 33–49; and Berthold von Schenk, "Factors That Unite Us: Protestant," in *Christians in Conversation* (Westminster: Newman, 1962), p. 61. The Protestant theologian Asmussen is quoted by Geiselmann: "Not Scripture but preaching came first . . . . Scripture developed out of the apostolic proclamation. This means nothing less than this, that the New Testament itself is a part of 'tradition,' whether or not one calls it by that name" (Josef Geiselmann, *"Das Konzil von Trient über das Verhältnis der Heiligen Schrift und der nicht geschrieben Traditionen,"* in Schmaus, ed., *op. cit.,* p. 131).

[19] See Congar, *op. cit.,* p. 217; see also A.-M. Dubarle, "Introduction to Holy Scripture," in A.-M. Henry, ed., *Introduction to Theology,* tr. William Story (Theology Library, vol. I; Chicago: Fides, 1954), p. 65.

[20] Rahner, *op. cit.,* p. 37.

[21] His study was published in German in *Una Sancta* in 1956; it was translated into French in *Istina,* V (1958), 197–214, under the title *"Un Malentendu éclairci: La Relation 'Écriture-Tradition' dans la Théologie catholique,"* and was summarized in *Theology Digest,* VI (Spring, 1958), 73–78. Essentially the same material with development of the post-Tridentine era was incorporated into the longer essay (pp. 123–206) in Schmaus already cited. Previous to Geiselmann's study of Trent, the most notable recent works were Joaquim Salaverri, *"La Tradición valorada como Fuente de la Revelación en el Concilio de Trento,"* *Estudios Eclesiásticos,* XX (January, 1946), 33–61; Edmond Ortigues, *"Écriture et Traditions apostoliques au Concile de Trente,"* *Recherches de Science religieuse,* XXXVI (April, 1949), 270–299; and W. Koch, *"Der Begriff Traditiones im Trienter Konzildekret der Sessio iv,"* *Theologische Quartalschrift,* CXXXII (January-April) 1952), 46–61, 193–211.

[22] Bouyer, *op. cit.,* p. 191.

[23] Karl Adam, *The Christ of Faith,* tr. Joyce Crick (New York: Pantheon, 1957), p. 9.

[24] See Otto Semmelroth, *"Die Heilige Schrift als Glaubensquelle,"* *Stimmen der Zeit,* CLXI (January, 1958), 37; Gustave Weigel: "Nor need we reject the Protestant formula, scripture alone, provided we understand the phrase to mean the scriptures kept alive by the enveloping living

tradition" (*Catholic Theology in Dialogue* [New York: Harper, 1961], p. 92); and John Sweeney: "For time and time again the scholastic theologians said that the source of Christian revelation is *scriptura sola*; revelation is to be found *solum in scriptura*" ("The Challenge to Theology," *Proceedings: Thirteenth Annual Convention, Catholic Theological Society of America,* XIII [1958], p. 183). It need hardly be said that these three authors go on to develop the meaning of *scriptura sola* and to contrast it with the Protestant view.

[25] Thus it is that the Protestant theologian Robert McAfee Brown writes that "a Catholic notion of Tradition being the faithful interpretation of Scripture . . . is certainly patent of a Protestant interpretation" ("Tradition as a Protestant Problem," *Theology Today,* XVII [January, 1961], 451 ff.); but he goes on to face the fact that an infallible Church makes the meaning of *scriptura sola* quite different.

[26] Paul de Vooght points out that not only is the whole of revelation not accessible to the Catholic by Scripture alone but also that no single truth of revelation is so available (*"Écriture et Tradition d'après des Études catholiques récentes,"* Istina, [April, 1958], 191).

[27] See Otto Karrer: "Holy Scripture is for all Christians the binding norm for the Church's tradition" (in Cullmann and Karrer, eds., *op. cit.,* p. 155).

[28] Maurice Bévenot, "Tradition, Church and Dogma," *Heythrop Journal,* I (January, 1960), 40.

[29] Oscar Cullmann criticizes "Catholics, Gnostics and Illuminists" for not letting Scripture be the "sufficient norm" for the Church's teaching (*La Tradition* [Neuchâtel: Delachaux et Niestlé, 1953], p. 37). At the same time, Rahner can speak of Scripture as a "univocally binding and real norm, valid also for the later Church" (*op. cit.,* p. 51, n. 31).

[30] *Acta Apostolicae Sedis,* XLII (1950), 567.

[31] Baumgartner, *op. cit.,* pp. 182–183; see also René Latourelle, *"Église et Parole,"* Sciences ecclésiastiques, XIV (May, 1962), 201; and A. Leonard, *"La Foi, Principe fondamental du Développement du Dogme,"* Revue des Sciences philosophiques et théologiques, XLII (April, 1958), 285. The distinction between *regula fidei proxima* and *regula fidei remota* is useful here if it is understood properly.

[32] Heinrich von Bacht says, "The Church submits itself to the word of God and to his Spirit and will be but a faithful servant to the word and a willing organ for his Spirit" (*"Tradition als menschliches und theo-*

logisches Problem," *Stimmen der Zeit,* CLIX [January, 1957], 300). See also also Josef Geiselmann "*Die Tradition,*" in Feiner, Trütsch, and Böckle, eds., *op. cit.,* p. 103.

[33] G. Dejaifve, "*Bible, Tradition, Magistère dans la Théologie catholique,*" *Nouvelle Revue théologique,* LXXVIII (February, 1956), 146. See also Bouyer: "The very thing that Protestants affirm about the supreme authority, unique of its kind, of Scripture is likewise affirmed by the Church of today, as always without reserve and with unequalled precision" (*op. cit.,* p. 132).

[34] Compare Daniélou, *op. cit.,* p. 287, and Oscar Cullmann, *The Early Church,* ed. A. J. B. Higgins (Philadelphia: Westminster, 1956), pp. 87 ff.

[35] George Tavard, "Tradition and Scripture," *Worship,* XXXV (May, 1961), 379–380.

[36] Henry St. John, "The Authority of Doctrinal Development," *Blackfriars,* XXXVI (1955), 376.

[37] Joseph Ratzinger, "*Offenbarung, Schrift, Überlieferung,*" *Trierer theologische Zeitschrift,* LXVII (January, 1958), 27.

[38] Josef Geiselmann, "Scripture, Tradition and the Church: An Ecumenical Problem," in Callahan, Oberman, and O'Hanlon, *op. cit.,* pp. 58–60; Congar, *op. cit.,* p. 75; and Werner Bulst, *Offenbarung* (Düsseldorf: Patmos, 1960), pp. 18–28.

[39] See Rahner, *op. cit.,* p. 35. According to the writers under discussion, the Protestant writer Jaroslav Pelikan misplaces the "crucial question": "The crucial question is whether the New Testament exhausts the apostolic tradition or whether the development of the Church's life and teaching after the New Testament is also an exhibit of the primitive tradition supplementing the witness of the New Testament. If the latter is the case, then the authority of the apostles extends beyond the first century and comprehends the continuing apostolic tradition of all the centuries. Hence the teaching of the Church Fathers is an indispensable part of Roman Catholic theology" (Jaroslav Pelikan, *The Riddle of Roman Catholicism* [New York: Abingdon, 1959], p. 194). The theologians I am citing here would object that this misconceives the role of the magisterium, which is not to preserve the nonscriptural traditions and justify their apostolicity by patristic quotations but rather to interpret authoritatively the apostolic witness to revelation which is just as necessary

whether the Scriptures are complete or incomplete as regards the contents of the Christian faith.

[40] Congar, *op. cit.*, p. 75. See also Henry St. John, "Bible and Tradition," *Blackfriars,* XXXIX (August, 1958), 302.

[41] Cullmann, *The Early Church,* p. 88. Other Protestant writers are quick to agree that there is no esoteric tradition in the early church; see J. K. S. Reid *The Authority of Scripture* (London: Methuen, 1957), p. 140, and R. Hanson: "We may therefore take it as definitely proved from historical evidence that the Roman Catholic conception of the existence from the earliest period of an authentic tradition of doctrine, independent from Scripture, orally transmitted in the Church, is an illusion, a figment" ("The Church and Tradition in the Pre-Nicene Fathers," *Scottish Theological Journal,* XII [January, 1959], 25). The question which it is legitimate to ask, however, is whether this is the "Roman Catholic conception."

[42] See Congar, *op. cit.,* p. 75; see also Daniélou, *op. cit.,* p. 292.

[43] Daniélou, *op. cit.,* p. 287, who refers to the extensive study by Henri Holstein, *"La Tradition des Apôtres chez Saint Irénée,"* *Recherches de Science religieuse,* XXXVI (April, 1949), 229–270; see also J. N. van den Brink Bakhuizen, *"Tradition und Hl. Schrift am Anfang des dritten Jahrhunderts,"* *Catholica,* IX (1953), 109.

[44] Geiselmann, *"Das Konzil von Trient . . . ,"* p. 160; Semmelroth, *op. cit.,* p. 43.

[45] See Bouyer: "Not only did they know the Bible and make abundant use of it, but they moved in it as a spiritual world that formed the habitual universe of all their thoughts and sentiments. For them it was not simply one source among others, but the source par excellence, in a sense the only one" (*op. cit.,* p. 133).

[46] Congar, *op. cit.,* p. 75. For this use of Scripture in monastic theology, see Jean Leclerq, *The Love of Learning and the Desire for God* (New York: Fordham University Press, 1961), pp. 87–109.

[47] Yves Congar, "Holy Writ and Holy Church," *Blackfriars,* XLI (January, 1960), 16; Bouyer, *op. cit.,* pp. 232–233, has a note written by G. de Broglie on the argument from Scripture; and Hans Küng, *Rechtfertigung* (Paderborn: Johannes Verlag, 1957), p. 123.

[48] Paul de Vooght, *Les Sources de la Doctrine chrétienne* (Paris: Desclée de Brouwer, 1954), p. 149; Johannes von Beumer, in *"Das katholische Schriftprinzip in der theologischen Literatur der Scholastik*

bis zur Reformation," Scholastik, XVI (January, 1941), 24–52, had come to the same conclusion—see Geiselmann, *"Das Konzil von Trient . . . ,"* p. 161.

[49] See De Vooght, *Les Sources de la Doctrine chrétienne,* pp. 258–259; Congar, *La Tradition et les Traditions,* pp. 185–189; and Tavard, *Holy Writ or Holy Church,* pp. 22 ff.

[50] Tavard, *Holy Writ or Holy Church,* p. 174.

[51] Pelikan, *op. cit.,* p. 52.

[52] It is obviously impossible here to go into a day-by-day, point-by-point analysis of the Tridentine proceedings of 1546. The reader is referred to the studies of Trent mentioned in the first chapter and listed in the Bibliography. For additional bibliography, see Hubert Jedin, *A History of the Council of Trent,* tr. Ernest Graf (London: Nelson, 1961), II, 525–533, for Trent in general, and II, 52, for Scripture and tradition at Trent. All we intend to do in this section is note the most important and most controversial points germane to the question at hand.

[53] See Murphy, "Unwritten Traditions at Trent," pp. 242–243; Jedin, *op. cit.,* pp. 58–62; and Congar, *La Tradition et les Traditions,* pp. 211–212.

[54] Holstein, *"La Tradition d'après le Concile de Trente,"* p. 380.

[55] Geiselmann, *"Das Konzil von Trient . . . ,"* p. 161; Jedin, *op. cit.,* p. 73, n. 1, explicitly follows this account of the origin of the partly-partly formula.

[56] Pietro Bertano cites this passage of St. John, and Cervini, in the congregation of February 23, assembled this and twelve other scriptural and twenty patristic texts to prove this point. See Jedin, *op. cit.,* p. 75, and Holstein, *"La Tradition d'après le Concile de Trente,"* pp. 373–374.

[57] See Tavard, *Holy Writ or Holy Church,* pp. 173–174. This double channel of thought Geiselmann sees mirrored in the writing of John Driedo *("Das Konzil von Trient . . . ,"* pp. 147, 159). The difficulty of determining what the sixteenth-century theologian meant by tradition is well illustrated in the case of Driedo. Geiselmann finds the partly-partly formula in the *De Ecclesiasticis Scripturis* of 1533, and places Driedo among those who dichotomize revelation. Both Lodrioor and Murphy oppose this conclusion. Whereas formulas of Driedo out of context may sound as if he is using an extrascriptural source, that is, constitutive tradition, Murphy's extensive study showed that Driedo considered all truths necessary for salvation at least insinuated in Scripture. See Murphy, *The Notion of Tradition in John Driedo,* pp. 134, 137, 161; Joseph Lodrioor,

"Ecriture et Traditions," Ephemerides Theologicae Lovanienses, XXXV (April, 1959), 424–426; and Congar, *La Tradition et les Traditions,* p. 217.

[58] Geiselmann admits that the formula "had the consent of the overwhelming majority of the Fathers in the Council. . . . Only two of them protested energetically against the *partim-partim*" *"Das Konzil von Trient* . . . ," p. 48). Jedin believes that the astonishing thing is that Nacchianti was not met by stronger opposition (*op. cit.,* pp. 64–65). Nacchianti was reprimanded at the April 5 meeting for saying that it was *impium* to put tradition and Scripture on the same level. The example he gave of a tradition—praying toward the East—shows that the distinction of dogmatic and disciplinary traditions was not yet clear. See Holstein, *"La Tradition d'après le Concile de Trente,"* p. 379, and Jedin, *op. cit.,* pp. 86–87.

[59] Geiselmann, *"Das Konzil von Trient* . . . ," p. 151. See also Jedin, *op. cit.,* pp. 74–75.

[60] In Salaverri's study in 1946, he merely mentions in a footnote that the word *et* was put into the final draft "in place of the word *partim* of the first draft, against which only the general of the Servites had protested" (*op. cit.,* p. 48, n. 2a).

[61] Jedin, *op. cit.,* p. 87. Other writers trace it to Bonucci's objection in the same way: Holstein, *"La Tradition d'après le Concile de Trente,"* p. 384; Semmelroth, *op. cit.,* p. 40; and Dillenschneider: "The intervention of Bonucci was decisive . . ." (*op. cit.,* p. 91). This is, of course, one of Geiselmann's main points—see Schmaus: "Under the influence of the objections of these two Fathers of the Council against the *partim-partim* which the Council had put into the first draft, the Council replaced the *partim-partim* with *et* and left undefined the relationship of Scripture and unwritten tradition" (*op. cit.,* p. 162).

[62] Geiselmann, *"Das Konzil von Trient* . . . ," p. 163.

[63] An interpretation of Trent similar to the one given here is accepted by many theologians today. A long list of these may be found in Callahan, Oberman, and O'Hanlon, eds., *op. cit.,* pp. 36 and 59, and in Lengsfeld, *op. cit.,* pp. 122–123. Many of these have already been cited in this work—for example, Rahner, *op. cit.,* pp. 35–36, and Küng, *op. cit.,* p. 120—as also Daniélou, Congar, Semmelroth, Bouyer, Dubarle, Liégé, Schmaus, etc.

[64] See Johannes von Beumer, *"Katholisches und protestantisches Schriftprinzip im Urteil des Trienter Konzils,"* Scholastik, XXIV (1959), 249–258. See also René Latourelle: "It is certain that the primary intention of

the Council was to establish that besides Scripture, on which the Protestants relied exclusively, there is another source of revelation which is equally valid, namely, the living tradition of the Church received from the Apostles. They did not mean to say more than this" (*Notion de Révélation et Magistère de l'Église,*" *Sciences ecclésiastiques,* IX [October, 1957], 209–210).

65 See St. John: "The only independent traditions seem to have been interpretations and applications of existing doctrines and liturgical practices arising from them" ("Bible and Tradition," p. 304). Even the expression used when referring to the traditions in the decree—pertaining to faith and morals—does not necessarily have the same meaning as it has today. See Murphy, *The Notion of Tradition in John Driedo,* pp. 299–300, and Maurice Bévenot, "Faith and Morals in the Councils of Trent and Vatican I," *Heythrop Journal,* III (January, 1962), 15–30.

66 See Murphy, *The Notion of Tradition in John Driedo,* p. 3.

67 See Jedin, *op. cit.,* p. 87, and Geiselmann, "*Das Konzil von Trient* ...," p. 163.

68 Some state simply that the Council made no decision on the relationship; see Joseph Lecler: "The Council left unsolved the problem of their relationship. It was not then necessary to decide in favor of one school of thought" "*Église, Magistère, et Tradition,*" *Recherches de Science religieuse,* XLIX [July, 1961], 445. Others would seem to go beyond this position in saying, for example, that Trent sanctioned the view of the early Fathers; see Dillenschneider, *op. cit.,* p. 91. Tavard would seem to go still further: the logical implication is that the whole of revelation is contained both in Scripture and in tradition, though this could not be said because of the difference of opinion, but "the opposite conception that the Gospel is only partly in Scripture and partly in Tradition was explicitly excluded" (*Holy Writ or Holy Church,* p. 208). Some would say that Tavard is reading too much into the mind of the Council and that the Fathers of Trent could not be said to have *explicitly excluded* this conception, even if one thinks that it is implicit in their action. For this criticism, see Beumer, "*Katholisches und protestantisches Schriftprinzip* ...," p. 258.

69 See Geiselmann, "*Das Konzil von Trient* ...," p. 173, and V. Moran, "Scripture and Tradition: A Current Debate," *Australian Catholic Record,* XXXVIII (January, 1961), 21–22. In a study of Bellarmine, Beumer has pointed out that the *partim-partim* was not a thesis of Bellarmine and

Canisius; their concern was simply to oppose the Reformers. See Johannes von Beumer, *"Die Frage nach Schrift und Tradition bei Bellarmine,"* *Scholastik,* XXXIV (January, 1959), 20 ff.

[70] See Burkhardt, "The Catholic Concept of Tradition . . . ," p. 50. Geiselmann, in the earlier essays, said that the *partim-partim* in post-Tridentine thought was due first to Canisius; in a later essay, he places first blame on Cano ("Scripture, Tradition and the Church," p. 42).

[71] See Geiselmann, *"Das Konzil von Trient . . . ,"* pp. 194–199.

[72] *Ibid.,* pp. 200–206.

[73] See A.-M. Dubarle, *"La Bible et les Théologiens,"* *Revue des Sciences philosophiques et théologiques,* XXXIX (January, 1955), 73, n. 3; also Edward Rich, *Spiritual Authority in the Church of England* (London: Longmans, Green, 1953), pp. 136–147.

[74] John Henry Newman, *An Essay on the Development of Christian Doctrine* (New York: Image, 1960), p. 326.

[75] Reid, *op. cit.,* p. 129.

[76] See Bévenot: "The Church allows for more in revelation than what is contained exclusively in this rather disparate collection of letters and biographical sketches" ("Tradition, Church and Dogma," p. 41), as also Van Noort: "All agree that no single books contain(s) the whole of Christian doctrine, and so if in the ensemble they did cover it all, this would be quite accidental" (*op. cit.,* p. 147).

[77] The bull on the Assumption refers to *"sacris litteris tamquam ultimo fundamento nituntur"* (in *Acta Apostolicae Sedis,* XLII [1950], 767). See also Schmaus, *op. cit.,* I, 164–165, and Jones, *op. cit.,* p. 182.

[78] Congar, *La Tradition et les Traditions,* p. 217. See also Daniélou, *op. cit.,* p. 293, and De Vooght: "A tradition in a pure state which would not be founded on a fixed document would be led into the arbitrary, into caprice, and finally into disintegration" (*Les Sources de la Doctrine chrétienne,* p. 262).

[79] See Rahner, *op. cit.,* pp. 37–38; Gustave Weigel, "Catholic Ecclesiology in Our Time," in Callahan, Oberman, and O'Hanlon, eds., *op. cit.,* p. 189; and Bruce Vawter, *The Bible and the Church* (New York: Sheed and Ward, 1959), p. 76.

[80] De Vooght, *Les Sources de la Doctrine chrétienne,* p. 264; Holstein, *"La Tradition d'après le Concile de Trente,"* p. 390; and René Latourelle: "Church and word are two realities indissolubly united and mutually vivifying. The Church is at once that which convokes and that which

is convoked. Born from the word, it is at the service of the word and the sign of the word" *("Église et Parole,"* p. 211).

[81] Holstein, *"La Tradition catholique,"* p. 353; Schmaus, *op. cit.,* p. 166; Rahner, *op. cit.,* p. 51, n. 3.

[82] Leonard, *op. cit.,* pp. 277–278; Geiselmann, *"Die Tradition,"* pp. 105–108. Daniélou, points out that Catholic theology has not always insisted so much as the Orthodox churches upon the whole Church as the organ of transmission for revelation *(op. cit.,* pp. 288–291).

[83] Leon Cristiani and Jean Rilliet, *Catholics and Protestants* (Westminster: Newman, 1960), p. 115–116.

[84] In any ecumenical discussion, writes Geiselmann, this question eventually arises, a sign "that this is one of the fundamental questions, if not *the* fundamental question" *("Das Konzil von Trient . . . ,"* p. 125). See also on the Protestant side, Charles Moeller, *"Tradition et oecumenisme,"* *Irénikon,* XXV (1952), as quoted in Daniel Iturrioz, *"Tradición y Revelación,"* *Razon y Fe,* CLXIII (May, 1961), 454.

[85] See Otto Karrer, *"Ruckblick und Ausblick,"* in Cullmann and Karrer, eds., *op. cit.,* p. 155; Bouyer, *op. cit.,* p. 135; and Ratzinger: "Thus there results a new starting point for interconfessional dialogue" *(op. cit.,* p. 27). Even stronger is Geiselmann's statement, "The former opposition of Scripture alone or Scripture and tradition no longer exists, and the hitherto existing controversy over tradition is now a thing of the past" *("Die Tradition,"* p. 75).

[86] We have already remarked about this movement within Protestantism; many contemporary Protestants reject the separation of Scripture and tradition because it is a position "which was not that of the reformers, nor of the seventeenth-century theologians, but one which appeared with the diverse spiritualistic movements of the nineteenth century and which today is completely outdated" (Max Thurian, *"La Tradition,"* *Verbum Caro,* LVII [January, 1961], 49). See also Albert Outler: "The notion of a nontraditionary Church is an illusion" *(The Christian Tradition and the Unity We Seek* [New York: Oxford, 1957], p. 109). For other Protestant writers on this point, see Eugen Egloff, *"Die Ökumenische Haltung des Katholiken,"* in Cullmann and Karrer, eds., *op. cit.,* p. 48; F. J. Leenhardt, *"Sola Scriptura, ou: Écriture et Tradition,"* *Études théologiques religieuses,* XXXVI (January, 1961), 5–46; Henry E. Turner, *The Patterns of Christian Truth* (London: Mowbray, 1954); Pelikan, *op. cit.,* p. 235; Jenkins, *op. cit.,* p. 29; and Brown, *op. cit.,* pp. 430–454.

[87] Iturrioz says that there would be a great advance in the ecumenical dialogue if Catholics and Protestants really agreed on this point, but it is precisely this which "explains the affection and the illusion with which some Catholic groups have accepted this thesis" (*op. cit.,* p. 455). See also Gerard Owens: "It is certainly praiseworthy to remove any unwarranted obstacles to the path of reunion, but it seems questionable, to say the least, whether any approximation to the *'sola scriptura'* is a step in the right direction" ("Is All Revelation Contained in Holy Scripture?" *Studia Montis Regii,* I, [1958], 60).

[88] The Protestant reaction to the definition of the Assumption was for the most part a cry of betrayal. Says Patrick Fannon, "The ecumenical discussions of recent decades . . . tended to hide the basic differences we experience on this matter. Then came the definition of the Assumption and it was surrounded by a mass of bitterly disappointed literature which recalled this problem in all its starkness" ("The Protestant Approach to Mariology," *Irish Theological Quarterly,* XXIX [April, 1962], 128). See also Heinrich Köster, *"De Novo Dogmate Mariano quid Protestantes Germaniae sentiant,"* *Marianum,* XVII (1955), 37–55; Richard Baepler, "Scripture and Tradition in the Council of Trent," *Concordia Theological Monthly,* XXXI (June, 1960), 358–359; and Walter von Loewenich, *Modern Catholicism,* tr. Reginald Fuller (New York: St. Martin's, 1959), pp. 202–219, who says, "Such terms of expression as 'rather free' and the 'ultimate foundation' are clear proof that the bull makes no serious attempt at scriptural proof" (p. 135). Cullmann agrees that the Church has in fact abandoned the Scriptures in practice if not in theory: "She does not concern herself with giving it a scriptural basis" (*La Tradition,* p. 39).

[89] Davis, *op. cit.,* p. 282; see also Dillenschneider: "Professor Geiselmann has since established that the question is not subject to debate in view of the fact that the critical publication of the Acts of the Council of Trent determines for us the definitive thought of the Fathers on this subject" (*op. cit.,* p. 91).

[90] See Holstein: *"Many,* with just cause, rose up against a text which said that Scripture contained only a 'part' of the word of God" (*"La Tradition catholique,"* p. 350). See also Sweeney: "This form of the text (*partim-partim*), however, was not accepted on the plea of many that its wording discredited an undeniably Catholic position that held the inspired Scriptures to contain the whole of divine revelation. This plea was successful" (*op. cit.,* p. 182). The theologians I am referring to in this

chapter say that it is hardly exact to say that *many* were opposed to the formula.

[91] Henry Lennerz, "*Scriptura et Traditio,*" *Gregorianum,* XLII (July, 1961), 522. The late Professor Lennerz wrote two other recent articles on this same question: "*Scriptura Sola,*" *Gregorianum,* XL (January, 1959), 38–53, and "*Sine Scripto Traditiones,*" *Gregorianum,* XL, (April, 1959), 624–635. All three concentrate on the Council of Trent and the interpretation of Trent by Geiselmann.

[92] Moran, *op. cit.,* pp. 18–19, referring to the acts of the Council, I, 382.

[93] See Andrés Ibañez Arana, "*Escritura y Tradición en el Concilio de Trento,*" *Lumen,* VII (July, 1958), 341.

[94] Geiselmann, "*Das Konzil von Trient . . . ,*" p. 151.

[95] See Ibañez Arana, *op. cit.,* pp. 340–341; Lennerz, "*Scriptura Sola,*" p. 47; and Koch: "This opinion met with sharp opposition and a series of scriptural and patristic texts as proof of the existence and necessity of traditions" (*op. cit.,* p. 61).

[96] Ibañez Arana says, "So ended the affair of the bishop of Chioggia. His statement was considered scandalous; he was refuted; he admitted the existence of traditions not contained in Scripture and he did not again manifest his opposition to what was contained in the decree" (*op. cit.,* p. 341).

[97] Iturrioz, *op. cit.,* p. 468; Ibañez Arana, *op. cit.,* p. 342; Lennerz, "*Sine Scripto Traditiones,*" pp. 626–628.

[98] A. Spindeler, "*Pari pietatis affectu. Das Tridentinum über Heilige Schrift und apostolische Überlieferungen,*" *Theologie und Glaube,* LI (March, 1961), 177–178; see also Ibañez Arana, *op. cit.,* p. 343, and Lennerz, "*Scriptura Sola,*" p. 51.

[99] Even Johannes von Beumer, who is not without sympathy for the position outlined in Chapter 2, thinks that there is no essential difference between the wording of the first decree and the final one.

[100] Lennerz, "*Scriptura et Traditio,*" pp. 518–519.

[101] Lennerz wrote, "For what is in Holy Scripture is 'written'; what is in these traditions is 'unwritten.' Something cannot be 'written,' that is, found in Scripture, and at the same time be 'unwritten,' that is, not found in Scripture. These terms are exclusive: either written or not written" (*ibid.,* p. 632–3). Spindeler charges that Rahner judges Lennerz wrongly on this point by saying that he " 'concludes' from the Tridentine definition that there are revealed truths which are in no way contained in Scripture"

(Spindeler, *op. cit.,* p. 178, n. 10). On the contrary, insists Spindeler, no conclusions had to be drawn from the Council's decree: "Trent said it explicitly."

[102] G. Rambaldi, *"Un Texto del franciscano Andrés de Vega sobre la Tradición,"* Estudios Eclesiásticos, XXXIII (October, 1959), 431; see also his *"In Libris scriptis et sine scripto traditionibus,"* Antonianum, XXXV (January, 1960), 88–94.

[103] Bévenot, "Tradition, Church and Dogma," p. 38. In a review of Tavard's *Holy Writ or Holy Church,* Bévenot writes: "The trouble is that this book is dominated by Prof. Geiselmann's unfortunate interpretation of the Council of Trent's decree. This interpretation was refuted last year by H. Lennerz. . . . The author reproduces it here and in spite of the contrary evidence, concludes his account by saying that at the council 'the conception that the Gospel is only partly in Scripture and partly in Tradition was explicitly excluded.'" (in *Theological Studies,* XXI [September, 1960], 485).

[104] See B. C. Butler, *The Church and the Bible* (Baltimore: Helicon, 1960), p. 31; Benjamín Martín, *"La Sagrada Escritura y la Tradición apostólica,"* Cultura Bíblica, XV (January, 1958), 23; see also the conclusions of Ignacio Riudor's study of the Fathers and tradition, summarized in Cándido Pozo, *"La Tradición en la XXI Semana española de Teología,"* Estudios Eclesiásticos, XXXVII (April, 1962), 219–221.

[105] G. Geenen, "The Place of Tradition in the Theology of Saint Thomas," *Thomist,* XV (January, 1952), 123–125; Geenen lists eight texts as examples of St. Thomas's use of (constitutive) tradition. The author says that St. Thomas does not argue directly from such tradition because of the medieval technique of arguing from a text; true, the only conclusive text is a text from Scripture, but this does not exclude tradition as a source of revelation. To a claim of Richardson and Schweitzer that "Anglican divines would have agreed with Aquinas that nothing was to be received as necessary to salvation which could not be proved by most certain warrants of Holy Scripture," the Catholic critic C. Lattey answers, "Nor does Aquinas require 'most certain warrants of Holy Scripture' before accepting any doctrine, though he (mistakenly) does require some warrant" (review of Alan Richardson and William Schweizer, *Biblical Authority for Today,* in *Scripture,* V [July, 1952], 80). See also the summary of Manuel Miralles, *"El concepto de Tradición en Santos Tomás,"* in Pozo, *op. cit.,* p. 222.

[106] Lennerz, *"Scriptura Sola,"* pp. 40–43. Ibañez Arana says that he is preparing a work to show that "all the theological schools admitted, in one form or another, the doctrine which the great majority of the Council Fathers and theologians were to defend" (*op. cit.,* p. 344). See also the study of Vincente Gil, *"Tradición desde Vitoria a Trento,"* in Pozo, *op. cit.,* p. 225.

[107] Moran, *op. cit.,* pp. 16–18. For a study of Catholic thought on this question previous to the Vatican Council, see Daniel Iturrioz, *"Tradición y Revelación en el Concilio Vaticano y su Época,"* Estudios Eclésiasticos, XXXVII (April, 1962), 171–217.

[108] Owens, *op. cit.,* p. 60.

[109] Spindeler, *op. cit.,* p. 179; Butler, *op. cit.,* p. 47; Van Noort, *op. cit.,* p. 153; Bévenot, "Tradition, Church and Dogma," pp. 39–41; Owens, *op. cit.,* p. 60. Besides the canonicity of the sacred books and the institution of the sacraments by Christ, Lennerz gives as other examples of extra-scriptural truth the baptism of infants, the perpetual virginity of Mary, the imprinting of the sacramental character, the *filioque,* and the veneration of images (*"Scriptura Sola,"* p. 52).

[110] As, for example, in Daniélou: "What is essential in the sacraments: the pouring of water and the words of baptism, the formula of consecration, is at the same time in both Scripture and tradition" (*op. cit.,* p. 294).

[111] Spindeler, *op. cit.,* p. 179.

[112] Burkhardt, "The Catholic Concept of Tradition," pp. 70–75.

[113] Anthony Stevenson, "The Development and Immutability of Christian Doctrine," *Theological Studies,* XIX (December, 1958), 530.

[114] Spindeler, *op. cit.,* pp. 178–179. Eugene Burke agrees that the doctrines of Mariology would seem to require a modification of Geiselmann's theory; see his "The Use of Sacred Scripture as a Locus Theologicus," in *Proceedings: Fourteenth Annual Convention, Catholic Theological Society of America,* XIV (1960), 68.

[115] Butler writes, "It therefore seems that we must call in the evidence of the 'unwritten' tradition in order that the scope and limits of the canon of Scripture may be decided by the Church" (*op. cit.,* p. 47). P. Henry writes that there is much in favor of the theory that all revelation is in Scripture, though in the fixing of the canon *sola scriptura* is inoperant, in A. Robert and A. Tricot, eds., *Initiation Biblique* [3rd ed.; Paris: Desclée, 1954], p. 972).

[116] Stevenson, *op. cit.,* p. 495. Compare Spindeler, *op. cit.,* p. 179, n. 11.

[117] Spindeler, *op. cit.,* p. 178.

[118] Geiselmann, *"Das Konzil von Trient . . . ,"* p. 204.

[119] Moran, *op. cit.,* p. 18.

[120] See De Vooght, *"Écriture et Tradition d'après des Études catholiques récentes,"* pp. 195–196.

[121] Says Vollert, "To deliver the deposit, the apostles employed both the oral and the written word, as occasion warranted. The truth received from them by way of writing is Sacred Scripture; the truth received by way of oral speech is tradition, taken in the restricted sense as distinct from Scripture" (*op. cit.,* p. 63).

[122] See Stevenson, *op. cit.,* p. 495; Vollert, *op. cit.,* p. 49; and Pozo, *op. cit.,* pp. 219–221.

[123] See Martín, *op. cit.,* p. 23; Butler, *op. cit.,* p. 48; and Bévenot, "Tradition, Church and Dogma," p. 41.

[124] See Butler, *op. cit.,* p. 49, and also Burke: "Certainly there is no reason for denying and there is good reason to believe that certain disciplinary and supplementary doctrines and interpretations would be transmitted by tradition without necessarily being in Scripture at all" (*op. cit.,* p. 68). All do admit that there are disciplinary traditions and interpretations of doctrines passed down outside Scripture; the question is whether there are revealed truths which are in no way contained in Scripture, that is, whether there are constitutive traditions.

[125] Note that most of the works referred to in Chapter 3 have been written since 1958, and many of them are from 1961–1962.

[126] Lennerz, *"Sine Scripto Traditiones,"* pp. 629, 630, 631.

[127] The original text reads: ". . . *puritas ipsa Evangelii in Ecclesia conservetur, quod Evangelium ante per Prophetas in Scripturis sanctis Dominus noster Jesus Christus Dei Filius proprio ore primum promulgavit deinde per suos Apostolos tanquam fontem omnis et salutaris veritatis et morum disciplinae omni creaturae praedicari jussit: perspiciensque, hanc veritatem et disciplinam contineri in libris scriptis et sine scripto traditionibus."* Note that the word *fontem* is singular.

[128] See Geiselmann, "Scripture, Tradition and the Church," pp. 49–50, and B. van Leeuwen, as quoted by Lengsfeld: "Scripture and tradition are, as Trent said, the manifestations of the one source" (*op. cit.,* p. 124). See also Congar: "Thus the canonical Scriptures and traditions are for us the two channels by which the source of the one Gospel comes to us" (*La Tradition et les Traditions,* pp. 209–210).

116

129 Lennerz, *"Sine Scripto Traditiones,"* pp. 632–633.

130 Murphy has shown that in sixteenth-century usage the expression *traditiones apostolorum* did not deny that these truths might be found implicit in Scripture (*op. cit.,* p. 126, n. 77).

131 Geiselmann, of course, would be excluded from this line of thought. I do not intend here to judge Geiselmann's interpretation but merely to indicate a trend of thought which appears in recent studies by Beumer, Congar, Lengsfeld, and others. Geiselmann, writing after the criticism of both Lennerz and Beumer, answers them by reasserting his original position; see his article from *Begegnung der Christen* (1959) which appeared in Callahan, Oberman, and O'Hanlon, eds., *op. cit.*

132 Congar, *La Tradition et les Traditions,* pp. 217–218; see also Lengsfeld, *op. cit.,* p. 125.

133 Beumer thinks that even if the *partim-partim* had been retained, the present theory would not have to be rejected (*"Die Frage . . . bei Bellarmine,"* p. 4). It would not be necessary to understand the wording in the same sense in which Bonucci took it.

134 Lengsfeld, *op. cit.,* p. 126; compare Jedin: "Infinite exertion had been required to crystallize this conception. . . . Above all, instead of defining the contents of tradition by listing individual traditions, the decree connects it with the uninterrupted succession of the officials of the Church (*continua successione*) while its authority—after a lengthy discussion this way and that—was given parity with that of Scripture: all else was left to theological speculation" (*op. cit.,* p. 92).

135 Van Noort produces numerous quotations which seem to show a patristic doctrine of constitutive tradition, but he admits himself that they are "not testifying to that point" (*op. cit.,* pp. 48–53). Lengsfeld criticizes Lennerz for quoting pre-Tridentine writers when they are speaking of other than dogmatic traditions; he quotes Basil and Augustine in connection with *consuetudines* and St. Thomas on the veneration of images (*op. cit.,* p. 125).

136 Congar says that Lennerz does not take account of this tradition which existed into the sixteenth century, as Murphy's study of Driedo has shown (*La Tradition et les Traditions,* p. 217).

137 See Rahner, *op. cit.,* p. 64, n. 38, and John McKenzie: "A mechanical concept of this revelation has always been unsatisfactory; and it becomes even messy when one admits, as one must, that the writers of the biblical books show no awareness of their own inspiration. Were others better

aware of it than the authors, and if so, how?" (review of Karl Rahner, *Inspiration in the Bible*, in *Theological Studies*, XXIII [March, 1962], 106).

138 David Stanley, "Concept of Biblical Inspiration," in *Proceedings: Thirteenth Annual Convention, Catholic Theological Society of America*, XIII (1959), 84.

139 Rahner, *op. cit.*, p. 66–67.

140 Jones says, "We might add that even the decision on the canonical catalogue may be considered only an explicitation of the apostolic commission recorded in Scripture—if we remember that 'apostolicity of origin' seems to have been the earliest criterion of canonicity," (*op. cit.*, p. 184). And McKenzie says, "The Church which wrote the books is alone able to recognize whether they are hers; and the revelation of their inspiration is the contents of the books themselves, which she acknowledges as her belief" (*op. cit.*, p. 106). Murphy compares this revelation to the knowledge of first principles in human reason ("Unwritten Traditions at Trent," p. 263).

141 For a development of this question and the various opinions connected with it, see Stanley, *op. cit.*, p. 84; Bernard Brinkmann, *"Inspiration und Kanonizität der Hl. Schrift in ihrem Verhältnis zur Kirche,"* *Scholastik*, XXX (April, 1958), 210–211; and Lengsfeld, *op. cit.*, 114–115.

142 Henry St. John, *Essays in Christian Unity* (Westminster: Newman, 1955), p. 103.

143 Bacht, *"Tradition und Lehramt . . . ,"* pp. 60–61; Journet, *op. cit.*, p. 26; Leonard, *op. cit.*, p. 284; Leo Scheffczyk: "The fullness of this revelation cannot lie in any fixed written words, but only in Christ himself" (*"Biblische und dogmatische Theologie,"* *Trierer theologische Zeitschrift*, LXVII [1958], 199).

144 Rahner, *op. cit.*, p. 74.

145 Karl Rahner writes, "Revelation is not the communication of a definite number of propositions . . . but an historical dialogue between God and man in which something happens . . ." (*Theological Investigations*, tr. C. Ernst [Baltimore: Helicon, 1961], I, 48). See also C. G. Extremeño: "Revelation is . . . a dialogue between God and man in which the realities of our salvation are communicated to us" (*"El Sentido de la Fe, Criterio de la Tradición,"* *Ciencia Tomista*, LXXXVII [1960], 589). Compare St. Thomas's saying that the act of faith does not terminate in the proposition but in the reality (II, II, q. 1, art. 2, ad 2).

146 Edward Dhanis, *"Revelation explicite et implicite,"* *Gregorianum*,

XXXIV (April, 1953), 190. The following paragraphs rely mainly on Dhanis and Rahner. But see also Bacht, *"Tradition und Lehramt . . . ,"* pp. 38–62; Burke, *op. cit.,* pp. 77–79; Clement Dillenschneider, *Le Sens de la Foi et le Progrès dogmatique du Mystère marial* (Paris: Academia Mariana Internationalis, 1954), pp. 39 ff; and Edmond Benard, "A Development of Doctrine: A Basic Framework," *Proceedings: Fifth Annual Meeting of Catholic College Teachers of Sacred Doctrine,* V (1959), 14–29.

147 See Bacht, *"Tradition und Lehramt . . . ,"* p. 59, and Rahner, *Theological Investigations,* I, 63 ff. Rahner defines the "formally communicated" as "the total meaning of the utterance in fact communicated and intended in the speaker's utterance, but neither by speaker nor by hearer always articulated reflexively and propositionally, or even capable of immediate articulation" (*ibid.,* p. 71).

148 *Ibid.,* p. 69. Compare Dhanis: "Thus the testimony appears as a word by which one is invited to believe what is signified by it" (*op. cit.,* p. 191).

149 The expression is from Ortigues, *op. cit.,* p. 296.

150 Both Dhanis and Rahner assert that if a truth is formally testified to by God it is definable, whether this truth according to our *logical processes* is formally implicit, virtually implicit, or implicit in some other way. Both theologians transcend the problem by approaching the question from the standpoint of what God intends to communicate and by making the distinction between the formally stated and the formally communicated. In Benard's exposition of Dhanis's ideas, he begins by distinguishing the development of dogma from the development of theology. He then says that the "virtually implicit" has no place in the former, and proceeds to an exposition of what is formally implicit in testimony. This may be essentially the same as Rahner and Dhanis, but there appears to be danger of a confusion without Dhanis's clear distinction of *formellement attesté* and *formellement signifié.* An ambiguity can arise because of the two possible uses of the expressions *formally implicit* and *virtually implicit.* While a dogma must be formally implicit—from the standpoint of testimony—it may be virtually implicit—from the standpoint of what is stated. Compare Dhanis: "This conclusion does not coincide—and it is important to emphasize this—with the opinion of some theologians who hold that the development of dogma would extend only to truths formally implicit in the apostolic doctrine, to the exclusion of those which are virtually implicit" (*op. cit.,* p. 197).

[151] St. John, "The Authority of Doctrinal Development," pp. 379–380. Compare Rahner, *Theological Investigations*, I, 55; Bacht, *"Tradition und Lehramt . . . ,"* pp. 60–61; and Jones: "The Church's knowledge of the Word then is not merely equal to the sum of biblical scholarship of twenty centuries. . . . The equation: Logic plus text equals theology is quite inadequate in the Catholic view because it leaves out the 'Spiritus suggeret omnia . . .'" (*op. cit.,* p. 187).

[152] This is what Journet calls proceeding from the gnoseological element of revelation to the ontological (*op. cit.,* p. 17). See Vollert "To supply for the inadequacies of logical procedures, recourse is made to the Christian sense as a means which God has made available to the Church for bringing out explicitly his profound design in the supernatural order" (*op. cit.,* p. 55). It may be remarked that this is the process which is so incomprehensible to most Protestants. To many of them, the *sensus fidelium* appears to be a new source of dogmas rather than the means of making the revelation which closed with the Apostles explicit.

[153] Rahner, *Theological Investigations,* I, 76.

[154] Compare Leonard: "The basic principle, the determining factor in the continuity of the development of dogma is the faith itself, informed by tradition and directed by the magisterium" (*op. cit.,* p. 286). See also Extremeño: "The magisterium cannot propose anything infallibly to the church which is not found in tradition, the rule of faith in the church. But this tradition . . . is manifested in the sense of the faith of the bishops, Fathers, Doctors, theologians, and simple faithful" (*op. cit.,* pp. 602–603).

[155] Journet, *op. cit.,* pp. 31–32. Compare F.-M. Braun *"La Bible dans la Vie de l'Église à la Lumière du Nouveau Testament,"* *Bible et Vie chrétienne,* XII (December, 1955), 39.

[156] Rahner, *Inspiration in the Bible,* p. 74. Compare Lengsfeld: "As soon as the material sufficiency of the Scriptures is acknowledged . . . exegesis attains in a special degree a new life, without which Catholic theology is condemned to become old and sterile" (*op. cit.,* pp. 127–128).

[157] Rahner, *Inspiration in the Bible,* p. 75.

[158] Compare *ibid.,* p. 35, 72; Tavard "Tradition and Scripture," p. 380; Lengsfeld, *op. cit.,* pp. 126–127; and Schmaus, *op. cit.,* p. 166.

[159] P. Henry, *op. cit.,* p. 973.

[160] Lecler, *op cit.,* p. 445. The same thing can be seen in the statement of Latourelle, who is evidently opposing the two-source theory but yet can say that Trent defined the existence of a second source which is equally

valid: "It is certain that the primary intention of the Council of Trent was to establish that besides Scripture, on which the Protestants relied exclusively, there is another source of revelation which is equally valid, namely, the living tradition of the Church received from the Apostles. It did not mean to say more than this. It did not pronounce on the question of whether there are truths which are in no way contained in Scripture" ("*Notion de Révélation et Magistère de l'Église*," pp. 209–210).

[161] When the word *source* is used in the second sense, then all Catholics must hold to a two-source theory. The Council defined that revelation can be found in "written books and unwritten traditions." Burkhardt says that "under the aspect of the mode of transmission, we may speak less properly of two sources of faith" ("The Catholic Concept of Tradition . . . ," p. 67). Not enough care is always taken to distinguish that this is a secondary sense of the word.

[162] According to the definitions I am proposing here, *two-source theory* would be a complete misnomer. If one were to use the word *source* only with this meaning, then every Catholic would hold to a one-source theory. One who defends constitutive tradition may balk at this terminology, which is admittedly that of the other side. Actually, the same distinction is made by Lennerz when he distinguishes between unwritten traditions and apostolic traditions (see "*Sine Scripto Traditiones*," p. 633). Stevenson tries to fix the terminology by regarding Scripture and tradition "less as two separate sources than as a single twofold source" (*op. cit.*, p. 495). There would be much to recommend the expression, but it does not seem to avoid ambiguity as well as the terms of Congar, Holstein, Van Leeuwen, Ortigues, and others proposed here. This may seem like quibbling, but the main point of an argument can hardly escape confusion when there is the slightest doubt about a basic definition. Whether the use of words proposed here is acceptable or not, the distinction of ideas is a necessary one.

[163] See Stevenson, *op. cit.*, p. 495; Burke, *op. cit.*, p. 67; Rahner, *Inspiration in the Bible*, p. 47; De Vooght, *Les Sources de la doctrine chrétienne*, p. 262; and Pozo, *op. cit.*, pp. 219–221. Note that I say both sides agree that the central mysteries of Christianity are in the Scriptures. One side says that all the dogmas can be made explicit from what is in Scripture; the other side says that some of the secondary dogmas cannot be so deduced. The fundamental attitude of each toward the Scriptures should not be different; both can recognize the unique position of the scriptural word of God, the written form of the apostolic *paradosis*,

wherein most if not all of God's revelation to mankind is contained. The Bible should not be considered as secondary or unessential by either side; the Bible is *the* book of the Church.

164 To one side this means that Scripture is not complete and requires oral traditions to supplement it. To the other side, this same statement means that Scripture is complete in that it contains the starting point for later doctrinal explication and for a deeper penetration behind the text of the Scriptures. Compare Butler, *op cit.,* p. 47; Leonard, *op cit.,* p. 284; Extremeño, *op. cit.,* p. 589; and Rahner, *Theological Investigations,* I, 63 ff.

165 Compare Geiselmann, *"Das Konzil von Trient . . . ,"* p. 204; and Bévenot, "Tradition, Church and Dogma," p. 39.

166 This may be the most surprising point of agreement and possibly the best suited to building a bridge of understanding. Obviously, those defending constitutive tradition agree to this, "that it must not be forgotten that the transmission of Christian origins was not confined to the New Testament writings. For a time oral tradition will have gone on and played its legitimate part alongside the written materials (Butler, *op. cit.,* p. 31). It may not always be realized, however, that those denying constitutive tradition can affirm something not entirely dissimilar. Henry St. John writes: "When the written tradition was completed and the depositum closed by the death of the last apostle, the unwritten tradition and the insights of the faithful in prayer and the study of theology combined to effect a deeper realization of the meaning of the written word (*Essays in Christian Unity,* p. 102). Likewise, de Broglie who is not at all denying the completeness of Scripture, writes: "What Catholics do not admit is that all this flood of divine word which issued from them into the world subsequently disappeared, except that part which they committed or caused to be committed to writing" (in Bouyer, *op. cit.,* p. 233). It may be helpful to recall here that the preservation and transmission of revelation is by the whole Church, and that the Apostles bestowed on the Church a living experience through the indwelling Spirit, which in the concrete life of the Church makes revelation clearer than the scriptural texts alone could. The point here is that both sides can speak of an extrascriptural tradition which comes from the Apostles and which completes in some way the written word. Compare Bacht, *"Tradition und Lehramt . . . ,"* pp. 60–61, and Ratzinger, *op. cit.,* p. 27.

167 This is perhaps an unjust accusation made against those who defend constitutive tradition, that is, that they suppose a hidden and esoteric

tradition. Although oral (constitutive) tradition may have been so conceived, it would not have to be that. It is not necessary that every dogma was explicitly formulated and told to someone by an Apostle. Constitutive tradition could be a complex of acts, ceremonies, and knowledge, which was absorbed into the life of the Church and became the means of later perceiving extrascriptural truths more clearly.

[168] Some who are on the side of constitutive tradition would refuse to grant that a starting point in Scripture is necessary for the defining of a dogma. However, many if not most of these theologians would be willing to agree with this because the practice of the Church seems to indicate that this is so. Their objection is with the fact that "a foundation is not a house, a seed is not a tree, and a convenient ground is not a dogma" (Spindeler, *op. cit.,* p. 178). Note how one side says that all revelation is in Scripture because a starting point can be found there for each dogma; the other side says that all revelation is not contained in Scripture because *only* a starting point can be found there. Both make use of the very same quotation from *Munificentissimus Deus: "Sacris Litteris tamquam ultimo fundamento nituntur."* Does being an ultimate foundation mean that it is there or is not there?

[169] Bévenot accuses Geiselmann of not meaning what he says because on the one hand Geiselmann says all revelation is contained in Scripture while on the other he says that tradition completes Scripture. (Bévenot, "Tradition, Church and Dogma," p. 39). It would seem, however, that one must be willing to grant that a word like *complete* can be used in different senses. No Catholic denies that tradition completes Scripture in some way; the question is how it completes it. The completion of tradition means to Geiselmann that Scripture needs tradition to be understood and interpreted although Scripture itself is complete as to its contents, that is, materially complete.

[170] Johannes von Beumer, "Das katholische Traditionsprinzip in seiner heute neu erkennten Problematik," *Scholastik,* XXXVI (April, 1961), 217–240.

[171] There are other writers who take this same approach to the question. Beumer's article is cited here as an example of emphasis on a point which is more or less implicit in some of the other writing on this question.

[172] Beumer, *"Das katholische Traditionsprinzip . . . ,"* pp. 238–239. The idea of tradition as the "homogeneous unfolding" of Scripture he attributes to Kuhn and Geiselmann. Whether Geiselmann would accept this

description of his doctrine, only he could say. However, the position which Beumer characterizes as a middle ground would appear to be reconcilable with the great majority of the writers referred to in Chapters 2 and 4. But Beumer does seem to shift the center of the problem from emphasis on the sufficiency of Scripture and the nonexistence of constitutive tradition to the unity of Scripture and tradition.

173 *Ibid.*, p. 240. It is difficult to understand how this would differ essentially from Geiselmann on this point. Geiselmann agrees with Kuhn that Scripture supplies the starting point and that Scripture and tradition mediate the whole Gospel under different forms: "Holy Scripture transmits to us the revealed truths of the Gospel, but tradition transmits revelation in the form of its interpretation and authoritative understanding" (*"Der Konzil von Trient . . . ,"* pp. 204–206).

174 See Hans Küng, *The Council, Reform and Reunion,* trs. Cecily Hastings (New York: Sheed and Ward, 1961), pp. 5 ff.

Index of Names